FROM PRACTICE TO THEORY

Roger Kenneth Cox

Grosvenor House
Publishing Limited

All rights reserved
Copyright © Roger Kenneth Cox, 2021

The right of Roger Kenneth Cox to be identified as the author of this
work has been asserted in accordance with Section 78
of the Copyright, Designs and Patents Act 1988

The book cover is copyright to Roger Kenneth Cox

This book is published by
Grosvenor House Publishing Ltd
Link House
140 The Broadway, Tolworth, Surrey, KT6 7HT.
www.grosvenorhousepublishing.co.uk

This book is sold subject to the conditions that it shall not, by way of
trade or otherwise, be lent, resold, hired out or otherwise circulated
without the author's or publisher's prior consent in any form of binding or
cover other than that in which it is published and
without a similar condition including this condition being imposed
on the subsequent purchaser.

A CIP record for this book
is available from the British Library

ISBN 978-1-83975-599-6

To Maximillian

CONTENTS

1 BRUM Family life in war-torn Birmingham – just as busy as in normal times; a small boy at school, and a father who combined design engineering with church ministry and air-raid warden. A move to Scotland.   1

2 BONNIE DUNDEE The shock of Scottish culture; four house moves and four churches in the city. A deviant path for my studies   6

3 AULD REEKIE Another move to the capital, and a puzzle on my father's motivation; a school provides an improved career outlook for me; yet another move to Greater Manchester.   11

4 NO MEAN CITY My move to Glasgow to study; I found and edit a student magazine, becoming involved with an international student charity; meet with lifelong character friends.   19

5 NATIONAL SERVICE From Aldershot to West Germany; life at a NATO HQ; organising an Anglo-German Club; should the EU have its own army? Leisure travel around Europe.   26

6 SIXTIES LONDON Break-out to the British capital, and the start of my first career; flat-life in Marylebone; meeting my wife and marriage, then moving to the suburbs; back to Edinburgh with one child.   34

7 OISTREHAM Return to Kent with two children, and to my present house; re-meeting old friends, to my wife's relief; at last, a girl child; the family obsession with worldwide travel.   50

8 RETAILING My experiences with Littlewoods as a trainee manager; the start of a retail marketing career with NCR; further experience with J. Sainsbury, British Bakeries, John Menzies, Allied Shoe and a retail Philips' subsidiary; financial training as a city retail securities analyst; the realisation that I needed a career change; the future of retailing.   91

9 TEACHING A move into the Higher Education sector with Holborn College, CMMS, LSFT, Schiller International University, London Metropolitan University, The Open University, Greenwich School of Management, Western International University, South Bank University and other assorted universities, colleges and "crammers"; the future of HE.   117

10 CONSULTANCY Setting up and running a conference business; training supermarket managers for Tesco, Asda, Morrisons, the Co-op and many others through the IGD; freelance management consulting and research; TV and radio broadcasting; guest speaking at retail sector conferences.   140

11 WRITING How I learned, through doing and applying skills and knowledge, to write six books; experiences with publishers, agents and other authors.   154

12 MUSINGS Further job searches; getting in and out of debt; coping with retirement; personal reflections on my life and on the many people I have met.   162

ILLUSTRATIONS – The Rev B.A. Cox, Mary, David, Winifred Cox/ Roger (left) in BAOR/ Liz/ Steph/ Simon, Roger, James/ Roger in WADS farce.   45–49

APPENDIX Quiz and answers. References.   199

PREFACE

One of the reasons for choosing the title for this autobiography was the quotation attributed to Taoiseach Fitzgerald "That's fine in practice, but will it work in theory?" This reflects, in a way, my plunge into retail site assessment, with no specific training and little advice from colleagues.

To an extent, this has affected the chronology of the memoir, coupled with my father's constant need to re-house the family all over the country. I have tried to format the book to make logic of the consequent, often rapid moves in time and space.

Thanks are due to Jane Harvey, who supplied details of my late wife's family, my son-in-law Matt, for his design and IT skills, Doctor Ross of the Guildhall Library in London, who provided background to some of the characters in the book, and to my many relations and friends who have also helped.

Chapter 1

BRUM

Early 1943. North Birmingham. German bombers, probably aiming for Vickers-Armstrong two miles away, had dropped a stick of incendiaries and an HE on our quiet road in Gravelly Hill.

By 9am, a biggish crowd, mostly made up of schoolboys looking for shrapnel, milled in front of a demolished house in the terrace. I was part of the search and suddenly spotted, in the gutter, the scalp of the old man who had lived in the house with his wife. I shouted to a couple of men carrying a huge hamper; they moved over and put it in with their collection of body parts.

I was seven years old but took this almost as a matter of course. After all, this sort of thing was happening daily. On the wireless, Tobruk, Berlin and, down the road, Coventry, the manifestation of war and its deadly consequences were clear. In the latter city, the ruins of its cathedral had been carved with the words (perhaps somewhat disingenuously): "Dear Father, forgive them, for they know not what they do". But heavy aircraft with "Bomben auf England" painted on their fuselages still came.

My adoptive father, a Brummie born in Aston (a little earlier than Ozzy Osbourne) worked at Vickers as an engineering draughtsman, helping to modify the design of Lancaster bombers built at the Castle Bromwich plant. Alongside that, he had been trained at Rawdon College in Yorkshire as a Minister of Religion and preached at the local Methodist Church. At night, he was the local street warden. Bert Albert Cox had met his wife, Winifred Jones, at Humber Motors in Coventry. Both had attended art college and, as a result, had produced many portraits heavily influenced by Alma-Tadema and Burne-Jones: I still have my mother's portrait of Lady Nairne in my drawing room, while Dad's rendition of Christ in the Wilderness has long gone. Incidentally, he used to tell many stories about his time after training for the ministry. While preparing for consecration at a County Durham church, he raised the cloth over the charged glasses on the table and nearly passed out with the aroma. He questioned the verger on the use of port wine for the benediction and received the reply, "There's no point in it, unless there's a kick!"

Looking back on this and the loving household they both created, I, Roger Kenneth Cox, was more than glad to have been chosen by the couple. This came about partly by the death of their first child, David. According to my new father, this had been due to the bungling of a paediatrician, and he maintained a lifelong grudge against the profession. But a year after my adoption, Mary was born, and after the war, another David.

I was about five when I was told that I had been adopted. This early revelation was probably crucial in forming my attitude – that it was perfectly normal. I was alive. For me, it reduced the common instinct to try to work out where I came from – the "Finding Nemo" syndrome. I just didn't worry about it. And, despite the war, I had my family and friends in the neighbourhood, at school and through my father's church.

Each school day, I walked to Ryland Road Elementary, about a mile through a pleasant suburban area. On occasion, we were shown government propaganda films from a van outside the school and once viewed a Spitfire flypast, thanks for our donations to its manufacture. On the way to the school, I went through The Oval, a small park which on its south side had a gap between the houses. This formed a way of getting from Gravelly Hill to Tyburn Road and the canal, where I often fished with friends. One winter evening, I decided to come home this way up a rather steep piece of wasteland. Halfway up, I found an older boy making tiny crosses out of thin twigs, apparently for a little graveyard on a flat space he had found. I stopped as he finished it off by placing in its centre a lighted cigarette as a sort of beacon. As I gazed at it in admiration, a couple of bigger boys came up and stamped on the little replica, almost obliterating it. They both ran off laughing, angrily pursued by the "architect". I kneeled down to try to rebuild the model from the bits and pieces left, only to burn my fingers on the cigarette. I often revisited the place, I suppose from sentiment. Place has always been important and, oddly enough, I have revisited all 10 family houses I have lived in during my life.

My mother took me regularly to a British Restaurant near the school for stodgy but palatable lunches of typically English "comfort food". More exciting were trips into the city centre for shopping at Barrow's, which smelled exotically of coffee and cheese – and the treat of the locally-made chocolate cakes. Marks

& Spencer was always crowded, as people travelled in on the blue and cream trams. In those days, for such trips, we children were dressed in tweed coats, with berets and gaiters on our legs. We were also controlled, like dogs with leather reins. One day, I asked to go to the lavatory and was duly de-reigned, and I trotted, alone, into the public facility. Inside, a man decided to urinate all over me, then make a hasty exit. Mum was completely unfazed at this, quickly wiped me down and called a taxi.

Dad might take me to the fish market where I learned about mussels, cockles and oysters, but more interesting was a brilliant miniature model maker, particularly of vessels like trawlers and destroyers.

Dad was also a good grandfather. When he was staying in Westerham with Mary, my sister, he told my son Simon of a 1917 Zeppelin attack at a Scout camp in Leicestershire where bombs killed several cows. One of Simon's friends, an expert on the Great War impact on Britain, confirmed the event.

My mother was born in Loughborough, and being an East Midlander, she was interested in the Civil War, much of which occurred in that region. She was particularly fond of the Cavaliers and, in a sense, she had that romantic mindset. Her husband, on the other hand, was a true Roundhead with a very pragmatic "Cromwellian" outlook, allied with a vile temper. He beat me, usually with justification, so I spent time finding suitable instruments of chastisement in the house and destroying them. When I became 14, Mum remarked at the time, "You are too big to smack."

In late 1943, he received a "call" to a church in East Scotland and accepted it. His motivation was unclear.

It meant giving up his engineering job and adopting fully his alternative career. Or perhaps it was a way of protecting his children (Mary was partially disabled) from the bombing. These thoughts obviously did not concern a seven-year-old. However, it promised adventure. I had won an old atlas in a class quiz and decided to do some research on where we were going. My reading was still in the formative stage. When I found the British Isles, I focused on the first two letters of the city we were going to: D and U. Being unaware of indexes at this point, I scanned our island group and decided that we were going over the sea to Dublin – an exciting prospect, as I had never seen open water except in Birmingham park ponds. Pointing this out to my parents, I enquired about shipping, until Dad pointed out Dundee.

It took 14 hours to reach the city by train at that stage of the war. I arrive black-faced, having hung out of the window much of the time, particularly when we stopped at the innumerable stations.

Chapter 2

BONNIE DUNDEE

I warmed to Dundee from the start. Like Birmingham, although much smaller, it is a no-nonsense place devoted to trade. As a result, it is not particularly pretty but today a solid post-industrial city with a university that wins top marks for student satisfaction. It is the place where the video game *Grand Theft Auto* originated and has recently opened a sensational branch of the V&A Museum. (The term used as this chapter heading refers, of course, to Sir Walter Scott's poem on the local earl).

Dad became assistant minister at Cleppington Parish Church of Scotland, serving a large congregation in the north of the city. Initially, we were lodged with a local doctor's family, but we soon moved into the top floor of the large church manse. This was in Albany Terrace on the slopes of the Law Hill, which dominated the city. This gave the family, including my mother and sister, a grand view of the "silv'ry Tay" as the local poet McGonagall described the river estuary. At that time, my father and I were particularly taken by the two or three Norwegian-crewed Sunderland flying boats moored across the river on the Fife bank. Also, being a keen ornithologist, he regularly put out bread on our balcony, which attracted an array of seabirds, including huge, belligerent skuas. Initially, I was enrolled at Roseburn School, a tough central institution, where my West Midlands accent amused the boys in my class, who spoke in quick, guttural Dundonian tones; my previous address was interpreted as "Mincemeat Road, Burning-ham".

One slight drawback was that billeted with us were two Polish soldiers. Although friendly and amiable, they infected me with Vincent's angina, a throat condition. I was taken to the nearby King's Cross Hospital and fed with penicillin on an orange juice bottle drip for a couple of weeks – a first taste of the NHS. My teacher at school got my classmates to write to me, and I duly corrected each letter for spelling and syntax.

I had, by then, been enrolled at the Harris Academy, sited on the riverside to the west of the city. School buses took my sister and I to it each day. Later on, when the family had located to a tough location in the north of the city, dominated by Cox's jute mill, Mary and I were inevitably accosted on Saint Patrick's Day by boys who asked us if we were Scots or Irish; our response that we were English always flummoxed them.

By 1946, it was time to think about the Scottish Qualifying Examination, the equivalent of the Eleven-Plus in England. The rector of the school, Doctor Peterkin, came round our all-male class and asked each boy what career they wanted. At 10 years old, I was, unsurprisingly, very keen about cars. I spent much time touring Dundee garages for car catalogues and copies of Glass's Index. I responded, "a car designer", and instead of going into the Classics stream, I was assigned to the woodwork and technical drawing classes. I remained at the head of the B division for the rest of my school career.

In the meantime, we had moved to a large house called "Devonside" in the north of the city, as mentioned in the penultimate paragraph. Here Dad became a "pastor", conducting services in the large front room and ministering to his flock in the area and beyond. At the same time, he preached at Ward Road Methodist Church in the city centre; he further supplemented his meagre stipend as chaplain to the then Dundee Royal Infirmary. Some years later, he became involved with the Scottish Congregational chapel in Hawkhill, an old section of Dundee near the university. Knowing that he had been a Baptist parson before I was born, I perhaps harboured suspicions about his motivation. This was the fourth church he had been preaching in since we had lived in Dundee. There were to be more churches in the succeeding years. Latterly, I did query this progression. "Well, my lad," he declared, "I'm seeking a sect which offers the governance I can happily accept!"

At school, I became interested in trainspotting, partly due to the Ian Allan series of books which listed the classes and operating numbers of the steam locomotives in the then four companies that provided Britain with train services. I used to cycle down to the Tay Bridge where both the LNER and LMS companies ran into their respective stations in Dundee. At that time, we could enter the engine sheds filled with parked locomotives and "spot" them. You were supposed to have a permit, but, of course, no 14-year-old would be allowed near such an industrial site today.

I wrote to the local newspaper, the *Dundee Courier*, complaining that the old 2-4-2 engines hauling local services needed replacing in the light of the formation of British Railways in 1948. I was surprised and gratified when one of the local MPs, Willie Gallacher, the only communist member of Parliament, responded with a scathing rebuttal that "new locomotives don't grow on trees".

Joining the Boy Scouts in a church that my father had nothing to do with, we soon had an inspection by the local commissioner. I was wearing a Gilwell woggle that my father, as a Scoutmaster, had been awarded at the Derbyshire Jamboree. I was ordered to take it off and to cease using it. I obeyed on the first injunction, but later in an Edinburgh troop, I resumed wearing it.

As a keen follower of the Dundee Tigers ice hockey team, I regularly attended matches with friends at the local ice rink. Like most teams in the popular Scottish league at the time, it fielded two Canadian players. Swimming at the harbour baths was particularly enjoyable, not only with classmates but when I could dodge into a shower among a mob of females of all ages wearing black full swimming costumes. Going to the Caird Hall with the school to hear children's classics like *Peter and the Wolf* was another reminder of how good Scottish education was 60 years ago. Trips to the Dundee Repertory Theatre (famous for actors like Richard Todd, Lynn Redgrave and Brian Cox – himself a Dundonian) might involve showings of *The Wind in the Willows* or a Scottish comedy. Another side to the city was illustrated by the Dundee grandmother, whose response to Kenneth Tynan's use of the "f" word for the first time on British television was "How nice it was to hear that sweet word on the TV."

I am sure he would not object to this irrelevant juxtaposition in a memoir, but one of my closest friends at the age of 13 was Douglas Cullen, a near neighbour when I lived in Albany Terrace. Douglas was the son of a local judge and he wanted to follow his father into the law. We used to play pretend law courts at his house, and I was usually the defendant so that he could pose as the cross-examining advocate. I was often invited to supper with him and his parents; I remember, guiltily, producing permanent boot scuffs on the cross-bar of my chair.

Ennobled as Lord Cullen, his distinguished career probably peaked with his chairing of the inquiry into the Piper Alpha disaster; this occurred when a North Sea oil rig exploded, causing many deaths.

I next saw Douglas when he came with an Edinburgh Academy schoolfriend to the manse we were living at in the north of the Scottish capital. My father had received another call to a Congregational church in north Edinburgh.

Chapter 3

AULD REEKIE

The turn of the decade saw the family moving south to the Scottish capital. Dad was staying with the Congregational church and he took up ministership at Granton on the banks of the Forth. It was one of several harbours in the city and was well known for the import of Esparto grass for the city's paper and flourishing publishing industries.

By this time, my brother, David, had been born and the five of us lived in a bungalow manse next to the church. Later on, having researched bursaries for the sons of church ministers, I was able to have him enrolled at Daniel Stewart's College, one of the several prestigious schools in the city. He joined its cadet force, but it was ages before I ironed his tam o' shanter to provide its proper sharp edges (a trick I learned during my National Service).

At my own new school, the problem of my future career path was partially solved by my helpful book-keeping and commerce teacher, who suggested that I take an economics degree. My favourite subjects were English, geography, history and art. Other key thought leaders in my development were Messrs McDonald and

Lucas, both among my favourite teachers. The former, who had suffered from PTSD produced while fighting in the Italian Campaign, often referred to the battles he remembered, unaccountably, by asking the class questions about it: one question was about the names of Italian aircraft involved, and as my father had given me spotter books of all the nations, both Allied and Axis involved, helped me remember Caproni and even Savoia-Marchetti. I was moved by his delight in my crass show-boating. The RE teacher called me "blasé", which I looked up in the dictionary and was defined as "sophisticated".

The church had a thriving Scout troop, so I rejoined (still wearing my illegal woggle) and became a patrol leader after earning several badges, including my favourite "Starman". Dad and I were both interested in astronomy and the sky. We both viewed two unusual night-time events together in our garden: a blue full moon and a performance of the aurora borealis – pulsating white searchlight-like beams coming together almost directly over our heads (unusual, not only in its format and colour to us, but also so far south in Britain).

During the mid-1950s, the great rock-and-roll invasion of popular music affected me like many young people. Access to it was difficult in Edinburgh (as opposed to, say, Liverpool). Films such as *Blackboard Jungle*, which featured Bill Haley's *Rock around the Clock*, teased appetite and, later, movies such as *Jailhouse Rock* (which I took Dad to see, but he was unimpressed) were palliatives. The tone of the BBC, as after the death of King George VI when we listened to days of dirge-like music, was only changed when its Radio One was introduced. We had to rely on Radio

Luxembourg on our "trannies", which were just being introduced. I had been brought up by my parents on the "Proms" and enjoyed, for example, Berg's Wozzeck as much as anyone. Additionally, I got to enjoy modern jazz, like listening to the Gerry Mulligan Quartet at the Usher Hall. A craze for be-bop (Parker, Monk etc.) developed through my great buddy Bill McLean, as told in Chapter 5.

Continuing my occasional habit of writing to the press, as a weekly reader of the "New Statesman", I sent a letter supporting a pro-Nationalist article, which commented on the attitude to Catholics in Ulster (this is in 1960, long before the later troubles). This resulted in a stream of Protestant literature from Belfast aimed at my father, a Protestant minister.

For two years, during college vacations, I worked in the local brewing industry. First, I was a tun cleaner at McEwan's in Fountainbridge. The beers were matured in large metal-lined tanks, which, when emptied, left a deposit that, depending on whether the contents were a stout or a pale ale, was of varying difficulty of removal. This was done using soda and cleaning utensils and necessitated using overalls and rubber gloves. There were occasional shrieks in the urinals as soda came into contact with private parts. Short breaks were spent in the "bothy", a term you were more likely to come across in Highland sheep farms.

The next year, looking for less exhausting work in a brewery, I joined Younger's in its old site, which is now occupied by the Scottish Parliament building. Here, the role was as a clerk following the drayman as he selected the various casks for each customer. The barrels, all wooden, ranged from pins (4.5 gallons) to hogsheads

(54 gallons). The drayman would shout out the number of each unit, and my job was to note these down in a special book for transfer to delivery notes. After a day or two, I decided that this was a charade, a meaningless exercise of extreme boredom. I concentrated more on sips of Younger's "Heavy", a dark and highly sugary concoction, which, at 19 years old, I rather fancied.

After eight weeks, during which I had filled in random numbers for each delivery, not a single complaint from any customer was received. Additionally, neither the comptometer operators nor the drayman had noticed the numbers were false. This confirmed my original suspicion that the job was a non-job because the only things customers were interested in were the gallonage, the beer type and whether the cask was secure (i.e. not leaking).

Turning back to Dad, he was a complex character and a stern father – which I have subsequently appreciated. He taught me chess, which I have passed on to my children. He was brilliant at crochet, and I still have examples of his place mats and larger pieces. As already mentioned, he was a competent artist and musician. He wrote copiously for his sermons and for the children's addresses given during Sunday service (I passed these on to an editor friend at Hodder, but she told me that they were old-fashioned and too didactic and humourless for modern tastes – he was most displeased to hear this).

Dad obviously had a substantial library, not only of ecclesiastical books and novels, which he received from a book club, but also an eclectic range of titles including Immanuel Velikovsky's *Worlds in Collision* and work from Aleister Crowley, the occultist and diabolist.

Incidentally, like his father, also an engineer, he was a hypochondriac. Noting that he took 25 different tablets a day, my brother Dave, who was working at a Manchester hospital, suggested he stopped the dosage in its entirety. The result, as Dave had surmised, was negative because the "medicines" were mostly either neutralisers or placebos.

The key point about the Reverend B.A. Cox seemed to be way ahead of the conventional interpretation of the gospel. First, according to Dad, this was not the Word of God, it was just the interpretation of the "word" by human beings. Following this, the "miracles" could be explained in simple terms, such as the "feeding of the 5,000" at Galilee was provided by the picnic food the day trippers brought with them to the gathering. Heaven and hell existed only in the feelings that people have for the departed – the Late King in heaven, Himmler in hell.

My father's explanation for our moves around the country were given a new slant, as revealed by my brother many years later. I was in Manchester, taking my sister out for her 80th birthday. She lived in a care home in Bury, renting her own room, which was filled with her collection of over a hundred dolls. Lunch was at the Midland Hotel in Manchester. I had checked that her gluten intolerance would be catered for, and we both enjoyed an excellent meal with Adam Reid at the French. Afterwards, I went to visit my brother Dave and his wife Alison in Levenshulme. During conversation about the family, Dave told me something I did not know, largely because I had been living in London. Apparently the church roof had undergone serious repairs during his ministry in Edinburgh:

The problem was that it had not been properly attached to the church walls, and this had been discovered by church officers. Strangely enough, a very recent report in *The Times* (10 April 2020) stated that "an architect who oversaw a botched extension has been struck off. Robert Lukas of HLP in Edinburgh told (his clients) from Germany who complained, that 'this is how we do things in Scotland'. The defects included a floor resting only on joists and a sub-standard roof, doubling the £140,000 cost of the work."

According to my brother, church officers dismissed my father from his post for allowing this to happen. Whatever the rights and wrongs of the case, and how blameworthy he was, his advanced views on the Scriptures as detailed above may have been anathema for some members of the congregation. Coupled with his penchant for "dressing up" for services – adopting a severe black "Wesleyan" frock coat at one time and a white "Anglican" surplice on another, or a purple stock – he was quite a character, bless him.

The upshot of all this was that the family moved, again, to greater Manchester. Dad had managed to fill a vacancy in an English Congregational church in Bury. The family – minus me, as I was living in London – moved into a terraced house in Ainsworth Road. Dave was still of school age and was studying at Bury Grammar School, while Mary was working at Remploy. Mum, in spite of the upsets of the previous years, was still a cheerful soul. When she was particularly happy, she broke into a little jig in the kitchen.

I was glad to be able to visit them all from time to time. I got much closer to Dave in particular, who had left school and was now working. He had taken up the trumpet and, like me, was interested in modern music from jazz to the Beatles. We cooked up various schemes to raise a laugh. I had been listening to the BBC Radio Children's Hour programme since the war, but now obviously saw it in a different light. We sent a request that "Uncle Mac", the distinguished old presenter, play Charlie Parker's single *Klactoveedsedstene*. When, years earlier, I sent a short story on motor racing to Scottish Children's Hour, with a supplementary request for *Loch Lomond* to be played after it, the story was obviously "spiked" and the song broadcast. This time, would you believe, no response at all. Another jolly jape was to enter a *Private Eye* competition to write spoof letters to the magazine *Time & Tide*. This was a fairly right-wing journal, long defunct, which was one of the *Eye*'s targets. I sent a mindless piece from a mythical Bury address. It appeared as the lead letter in the magazine's correspondence column. Unfortunately, I had forgotten to send a copy to the *Eye*, so did not win the £50 prize. Later, under the signature "Roadge", it did print a quote from *The Guardian* (expressed in those days as "Grauniad", for obvious reasons) in its "Pseuds Corner" section, which I was glad to see, still survives.

One day in 1963, Dave and I decided to travel to Manchester to see the newly released film, *M. Hulot's Holiday*. We set off in my car, the first I had ever owned, a 1959 Morris Minor registered SNK639, called "Snark" by my then girlfriend, Sandra, after the Lewis Carroll character. I had passed my driving test only a few months previously, but a large insect flew in the driver's window and I was completely distracted. The vehicle swerved and apparently hit a concrete lamp standard. Not unnaturally, I cannot recall any details, but when I woke up in Crumpsall Hospital (now Manchester Northern Infirmary), I was told I had broken my back (this was five years before Barbara Castle introduced us to seat belts). Fortunately, it was a fracture to the C2 bone near the neck, which meant wearing a neck brace after a week in hospital. Dave was more injured and suffered two weeks. I wept when I saw him – it was my fault. Fortunately, we both recovered. I was so glad when Sandra came up from London to see me.

In the meantime, Dad had expanded his pastoral care to three churches in Bury as congregations dwindled and ministers became sparse. He finally retired to a local care home in his late 80s. He made a friend his own age who was a pop music fan – which he just about tolerated as a classical afficionado. I drove up to see him quite a lot, and finally I saw him in Bury Hospital just before he passed away at 95. Mum died suddenly after a fall at 74. I was not able to come up from London to see her. They were both cremated at Rochdale Crematorium.

Chapter 4

NO MEAN CITY

I was standing at a urinal in the State Bar, just off Sauchiehall Street, and I turned to the wee man in the "bunnet" and remarked "This is no mean city". "Aye," he replied, "I' uz nae mean city, Jimmy." Of course, the term is the title of the famous book about Gorbals and its gangs in the 1930s, but it encapsulates the sheer toughness of Glasgow – very like another western port, Liverpool, with an equally impenetrable accent.

My teacher at Leith Academy had suggested that I take an external London university degree at a place near to Edinburgh. Scottish students have traditionally taken courses near to their homes. I joined the now unfashionably named Glasgow and West of Scotland Commercial College. This soon became The Scottish College of Commerce, which was eventually merged with the University of Strathclyde in nearby Bell Street.

I was 18 when I arrived in the city, and I immediately began a search for lodgings. I booked into the YMCA for the first day or two as I enrolled on the course and collected the usual bumf. In those days, student numbers were tiny compared to these days where universities are supplied with thousands of rooms for students in massive blocks. As mentioned above, many lived at home in their own cities, so it was quite natural for me to take up private accommodation; this allowed me to get to know native Glaswegians on their own territory. In one house, I remember a railway worker who was an ardent communist, and this provided the setting for many noisy debates. At the time, I was a Labour supporter and went with a French student in the same lodgings to hear Clement Attlee speaking at an election meeting.

I lodged in several parts of the city, first in posh Dennistoun where my landlady's husband sadly died suddenly overnight. I moved on immediately to Finnieston, near the "Big Cran", but was turfed out in favour of two Egyptian students. Fortunately, I ended up in Bridgeton with the delightful Miss Boyd in tenement flat off Glasgow Green. When the Hungarian Revolution was crushed in 1956, I went out into the local streets crying "Help for Hungary!" and collected many pennies. When I delivered the cash to the Glasgow University Union, I deposited with a veritable mountain of coins on a huge table – a sign of the great spirit of the Glasgow public.

Because Scottish "Higher" examination results were not enough to matriculate for a London university degree, my course in Glasgow took four years. The first year was spent in passing A Levels. The upside of this was that it provided much more time for extra-curricular activities. I got together a small team to help launch a rather glossy student magazine; it was called *The Pitt* after the street the college occupied. A prize for the best contributions was offered, which helped to provide content, while my assistant editor and I trawled the city for advertising. I preceded *Times* Editor Harold Evans' adoption of mixed typeface article headings by 10 years, only to have the policy reversed by my successor. At one shilling a copy, the magazine nearly broke even. I was asked to become the Scottish representative of the charity World University Service; this involved trips to London for meetings with its very attractive general secretary, Miss Rudinger. In order to help support WUS, there was also a need to organise dances and other events in the college.

One incident among these social events was based on a request by two Greek students. They wanted to give an illustrated talk on EOKA, the insurgent group which was fighting for independence in Cyprus and against British troops. George Carson, who was head of the students' union, asked my advice as to whether I thought this should go ahead in view of its political significance. I said yes, and the event proved to be thought-provoking and well received. It was followed, somewhat incongruously, by a display of Indian dancing. This was over 60 years ago, long before the phrase "no platforming" was coined.

George, who later had a career with Collins, the Edinburgh publisher, and I set up a foursome with two Orkney girl students. He later married his partner, but I had a completely platonic, friendly relationship with her friend. Of course, this news quickly crossed the 40 miles to Edinburgh, where my long-standing girlfriend Heather was studying at the teachers' training college. End of story. This turned out to be the only time in my entire life that I had my heart broken. I heard later on the grapevine that I was called a "teuchter", Gaelic for two-timer. In perspective, it was, at that age, best for both of us. I last saw her during the Saturday

Princes Street "social parade", when I was walking out with Jessie McGuffie, the publisher who later married Ian Hamilton Finlay, the poet.

I first met Bill McLean at college. He was in the year below me. My first impression of the thin, lantern-jawed man was his red face and the Guinness foam on his upper lip. It turned out that he had just emerged from a lunch-time session at the nearby State Bar. I immediately warmed to this wayward man, and we became close friends for half a century – until he was killed by a taxi in Byres Road.

Bill had been born in Ayr, son of a rail worker and educated at Ayr Academy. In those days, as I can attest from my own experience, the Scottish school system was rigorous but wide-ranging academically. In some ways, we were two of a kind. He was very eclectic in his interests. He introduced me to modern jazz, which could range from the Britons Jimmy Deuchar and Humphrey Lyttelton to Americans such as Charlie Mingus and John Coltrane. When he stayed with me in London, we became members of Ronnie Scott's Club at its original Gerrard Street premises. He was later a restaurant critic for an Aberdeen newspaper and collected Rennie Mackintosh furniture, such as his famous ladder-back chairs. Of course, we were regular visitors to the Willow Tea Rooms, just round the corner from the college, which Mackintosh had furnished. Not only was he, like myself, a bibliophile, but we both regularly visited the huge Stirling's Library, not only to write our essays. I remember helping him to put up a series of bookshelves in a library style in his flat; he was even worse than I was at DIY. As an Equity member, he was often on stage or television, acting under the name of William Irving; one of his appearances in the latter was in a Scottish-based edition of *EastEnders*, where he was an ambulance man. Both of us wrote poetry, some of which landed in *The Pitt*. On one occasion, after a session with his girlfriend in his Sauchiehall Street basement, she complained of being "awf'y sweaty, Billie. Huv ye a'thing tae wipe m'sel' doon wi'?" "Aye," says Billie, "There's some old poems under the bed."

Here are two efforts of my own: the first is pure, dated undergraduate cynicism, written over 60 years ago; the second is just the first verse of a poem written at the same time, with a modern addition because my memory failed on the original ending. Enjoy.

The Reader's Digest People

Hurrah! For the yeomen are leading today,
With medium-priced everything, paid for and gay,
And moderate squeals at injustices done:
All "Telegraph" readers, the crosswords such fun!
The yeomen of England, they really are nice.
Don't listen to "D.H.", he's so steeped in vice:
Like most intellectuals, he first runs them down –
Invents moral problems to make mother frown;
And Sex enters when they are ready to woo;
Don't speak of it frankly – that's rather taboo.
So wrapped in illusion, the secret thing rears –
It's all rather puzzling to many young dears.
For England! Their England! They'd fight to the end,
Better death from fall-out than being condemned
To dishonour, slavery and commissars, with horns,
Rudely drinking from red samovars.
But what of these good men who'd lay down their lives
To keep canals open, our flag in the skies
The Queen in her parlour and God in His heaven
And wish us all back to nineteen-eleven?
Well, Daddy's an officer in the Scots' Guards:
Establishment favourite, clever at cards.
And Roger's a manager – potato crisps –
"I'm making a packet" he laughingly quips.
Edwin's at the FO, though not very high,
Helping the Superior "fingers in pie".
And Sally's a mistress at a girls' private school,

She teaches them all, except not to play fool
Because they are English, they uphold the law:
Are good, Family People, who love a dog's paw.
And all the old ladies in Cheltenham and Bath
Would flog the young 'Teds' who have
left the straight path.
In good class districts, from Corstorphine to Cheam,
A great big kiss from our Jane to the Queen.
Now draw the chintz curtains to keep out the draughts,
And open the "Digest" and read out the laughs.

Peterborough to the Great Wen

Stacks in broken railings
Fence the pitted field
Where, by spade and oven
London's walls began.

Stories by Ackroyd and Inwood
Tell of Druids to present scene
And sing the great song
Of our City of any Dream.

Chapter 5

NATIONAL SERVICE

It was what service people call a "cushy posting" when I finally arrived at a large NATO group headquarters in the then West Germany. The relatively light workload as a clerk was not at all onerous and allowed plenty of time for other things. After a few months, anyone could gain a feeling for military culture. A friend at the HQ, Derek Norman, and I decided to produce an illustrated article for *Punch*. Derek had been trained at Chester Art School and latterly was an art director at J. Walter Thomson. (The submission was rejected, but Derek's caricatures and cartoons received a genial editorial nod).

As an introduction to the experience of National Service, some parts of the article are quoted here (copyright author). This forms a preamble to the nitty-gritty of my own postings. Incidentally, the most comprehensive study on the whole topic is Richard Vinen's *National Service: Conscription in Britain 1945–1963*.

"At entry, when training begins, the recruit experiences the abrupt transition from what might be called 'real' life to the Kafkaesque peculiarities of the soldiers' world: while singing idols donned great-coats and wept in the lavatory and others went 'over the wall', the great majority took the rather grim experience of military training in their stride, although with a good deal of grousing; at the other extreme, you could see it as a positive learning period and might even translate it into a career or a novel about it.

A strong impression many recruits have is that the main goal of military training is to produce a replica of a 'standard' soldier, an aim hindered by the battledress uniform, said by some to be the result of a mad anthropometric survey carried out in the rush days of 1914. Many young soldiers wanted to look smart, but the newly issued uniform often required drastic alterations. At the time, only ninepence of free alteration was allowed, with a private soldier on 28 shillings a week (£1.40). While a CQMS might describe a man in a normal issue as looking like a 'bag of s--- tied in the middle', a tailored blouse would face the 'straitjacket' jibe – a catch-22 situation. More simply, as described with my brother's Corps headgear, berets could be shrunk and boot 'pimples' removed by running a hot iron over a thick layer of polish. Fortunately, today's uniforms are more sensibly designed".

As a graduate, I was initially posted as a member of the Royal Army Service (now Logistics) Corps to Buller Barracks, Aldershot. Six weeks basic training readied us for Unit Selection Board, the first step to a commission. In the interim, officer cadets from the nearby Mons Barracks unofficially "interviewed" us. The chief interrogator wore a borrowed staff officer cap, while others wore berets and white collar tabs. A popular question was "What do you know about Kant?" This was easy to dodge, and I replied, "He wrote *Critique of*

Pure Reason", while responses of more gullible interviewees caused great merriment.

Subsequently, I went with my cohort to Barton Stacey, where I failed War Office Selection Board. I was sent with other failures to another Aldershot barracks filled with new recruits. This is where I learned the classic phrase used by "old timers" – "Git some time in, son!" Of course, we borrowed officer caps and carried out the same fake interviews with unsuspecting "squaddies".

Moving to Germany meant embarking on a troopship at Harwich, bound for the Hook of Holland – my first trip abroad. Our contingent was due to be billeted at an old Wehrmacht barracks near Paderborn, where we would be allocated our postings. The area was dominated by the tank training ground at Sennelager, with both Canadian and US troops in the vicinity. We regularly fraternised with them, swapping caps, regimental insignia and so on.

In a way, it was sad that I was the only one in our cohort to be assigned to Rheindahlen 2, the huge HQ in the West, near Dusseldorf. Obviously, it meant losing friends and acquaintances, so you had to make new friends wherever you went. But this was one of the great things about National Service and, for a middle-class boy, it was part of the social learning curve. To be sharing the same hut as an ex-prisoner from Carlisle Prison was revelatory – he was a great joker, at one stage secretly tying a condom filled with milk to my hangered battledress blouse. Nice touch.

This period, around 1960, was politically fragile in Germany. There was a constant fear that the Soviets would send their tanks from Russian-held East Germany across the plain towards the three Allied sectors. Although today this is viewed as farfetched, the military mindset then was a valid reflection of the time. Indeed, the four sector military systems allowed controlled reconnaissance of their own troop and arms movements in their zones. These "missions" were named after their nationalities e.g. BRIXMIS, SOXMIS and so on. In the Military Secretary's Branch, to which I had been posted at the HQ, we had a visit from SOXMIS officers. They were led by a Russian staff officer, and all the cleaners, who were mostly from East Germany, hid under the tables. (An interesting book on this topic is Tony Geraghty's *BRIXMIS*, Harper Collins, 1997).

War is conducted between states. States group together for defence and protection. This was the idea of NATO, whose key mission is to co-ordinate strike action against any aggressor if a member state is threatened. A fine example of this intention was the Rheindahlen HQ, where a dozen or so nationalities were represented. As an observer there, some anomalies and potential problems could be seen.

Every weekday, all junior ranks in each Command were expected to turn out for morning parade. This was conducted when I was there, allegedly by a former British troopship RSM, whose minions – and sometimes the RSM himself – would come round the barrack rooms to make up the numbers. The results were often comical. The Belgian troops locked themselves in their huts and refused to come out. The Germans, particularly the Unteroffiziers, loudly proclaimed that they were members of the Bundeswehr and thus excused. The British Army itself presented problems; infantry marching style is much faster than that of the Corps (e.g. The RASC).

That said, NATO has been conducting joint operations on the Russian border for years, but is a European army a starter? Apart from the fact that NATO has managed to keep European peace for nearly three-quarters of a century, why duplicate? At a recent Churchill Dinner held by the Westerham Society, the guest speaker was the former Foreign Secretary, David Owen. At question time, I just pipped a gentleman who was obviously aching to ask a question on Brexit, to pose the failure of the Dutch Command at Srebrenica to stop the massacre of Muslims (he was in the area at the time). My very swift supplementary was the usefulness of a European army; his answer was a flat "no".

At the Military Secretary's Branch, I acted as a corporal clerk, dealing with administrative matters such as the records of British commissioned officers serving in the British Army of the Rhine. The Military Secretary himself was a full colonel, reflecting the importance of the unit in the organisation. Over my 18 months there, we had three incumbents as MS. One of them, Colonel Gill, a much admired cavalry officer, sent me to the British Embassy in Bonn to help arrange the import of his two horses into the country. Quite by chance, my first house in Orpington was next door to a civilian MS, one of the civil servants who were replacing the military in the modern Army. Liz, my wife, and I became friends with the Jones family and were invited to stay at their large house in Viersen, near the HQ. Apparently, the house had been a brothel for German officers during the war.

Not that conditions 60 years ago were bad, even in the Army. The HQ was well supplied with leisure activities, but these were separated between those for the Army and those for the Airforce (the RAF operated several bases locally, such as in Gütersloh). It must be said that the latter facilities were superior, but soldiers of both arms and sexes could use both. They included swimming pools, cinemas, theatres, libraries, gymnasia, sports fields, running tracks, a medical centre and the NAAFI which were used by all. Budgets were liberal – you could order Peter Sellers and modern jazz LPs, books galore in libraries, or have free art tuition courtesy of the Education Corps, as I did. In June 1962, I had a letter published in *The Guardian* defending the social and educational facilities at the HQ. "Partly because of (its) 'clerical' weighting, the headquarters had one of the most popular Anglo-German clubs in BAOR. In 1960, when I was privileged to be its British chairman, the club had attendances of 60 or 70 at its Friday meetings, and many more when dances were held. Nationalities were evenly divided between British and German". A very successful "British Evening" was held in May 1960 in the Stadthalle of Rheydt, a nearby town (incidentally the birthplace of Goebbels). Town officials, a representative from the British Consulate in Dusseldorf and the commanding officer of the local British unit were present. This function was fully and appreciatively reported in the local editions of the *Rheinische Post* and the *Westdeutsche Zeitung*.

Through the club, I met Elvira, who taught me enough conversational German, and in turn, I tutored her in Business English. She passed an exam, partly by being able to impress the examiner with terms like "public utility". She told me that her father, an E-boat captain in the war, had burned her "Hitlermädchen" uniform when it arrived. By the same token, I met not a single person whose father had not fought on the Eastern Front.

One of the perks of living in Germany was the chance of European travel. It was amazing that the great majority of my contemporaries in the camp longed to travel back home during any leave we were granted. Derek and I spent a week in Copenhagen sightseeing and visiting art galleries, also taking a day ferry to Malmö. One of our more affluent colleagues who owned a red Karmann-Ghia drove the four of us to Paris. We travelled through the Battle of the Bulge area, and in Bastogne, I think it was, we saw an American tank mounted on a plinth at a road junction. Later on, we stopped in Rheims at 5.30 in the morning; standing at the porch of the cathedral in the quiet, only broken by a market stall-holder pushing his cart over the cobbles, was an experience that remains with me. France had just remonetised its currency, with the new franc replacing the old, which had exchanged with sterling for about 1,000 to a pound. Incidentally, the German DM/£ rate was 12 at this time. Certainly, the new French rate simplified paying for meals; one restaurant on the Left Bank that we did not patronise was empty when we entered, so we decided to leave – the patron tried to delay us by repeatedly playing our national anthem on the piano.

My favourite *Carry on* film is *Carry On Sergeant*, the first in the series. The story is more serious and arguably less amusing than its successors. Kenneth Williams, for example, plays a sensible character with an economics degree. This may be partly due to the fact that the phrase that launched the series is commonly heard on parade grounds, while the subsequent films have turned it into the common meaning of general chaos.

A minor actor in the film was Don McCorkindale, a colleague at Rheindahlen. A natural comedian and a very good actor, he was a much-needed entertainer on camp. More seriously, he claimed to be the godson of Freddie Mills, the champion heavyweight boxer who became famous after the war. Sadly, Freddie died relatively young, in 1962. In retirement, he had invested in other areas of show business and owned a popular club in Soho. At that time, the area was the proverbial "den of thieves" and Freddie was found one night in his car with a gunshot in his head. Suicide was the verdict in the investigation, but a subsequent documentary film challenged this. Don was interviewed in *Who killed Freddie Mills?* along with other friends and colleagues, to discuss alternative scenarios, such as that he had been murdered. The case remains another underworld mystery.

Overall, I enjoyed my time in the Army, particularly being abroad. One minor perk of the latter, in those days, was being able to buy banned books, such as Henry Miller's *Tropic of Cancer* and Vladimir Nabokov's *Lolita* in Paris and Copenhagen and smuggling them successfully through Customs. The German people were as friendly as Brits except, perhaps, on the occasion when, in an Essen swimming pool, a group of youths shouted, "Gott save ze Kveen!" at me.

Seriously, the experience has left me with a deep respect for the British Army and its traditions and long history. This is coupled with a concern, already hinted at in this chapter, for the future strength and health of our vital defence capability.

Chapter 6

SIXTIES LONDON

When I returned home to Edinburgh after National Service, I started my first full-time job in the commercial environment with the Littlewoods Stores Group at its Edinburgh Branch. Prior to this, I had been a "Saturday boy" at Patrick Thomson, a House of Fraser store on North Bridge. These experiences paved the way for my first career in the distribution sector (see relevant chapter).

At the time, the rest of the family were poised to move, again, to Greater Manchester. This is when my thoughts turned to London (after all, I had been born in Croydon). Here were major chances of jobs, new experiences and, hopefully, more money. That was the plan.

I arrived in London in January 1962 to take up a post with the National Cash Register Company (NCR). Initially, I lodged in Miss Bird's big house in West Hampstead. There I met another NCR employee, Derek Balmforth, who became a lifelong friend. We were part of a group of young businessmen involved in various fields. The West End was easily accessible on the Bakerloo Tube line, but we did not all rush off to sample the delights of Soho, we spent most evenings playing poker.

After a year or so, many of us moved on and I found a bed-sit in nearby, cheaper Cricklewood – this area later found fame in the BBC's fantasy series *Good Night, Sweetheart*. Bill McLean, my Glasgow friend, used to come and stay with me, largely to visit Ronnie Scott's to hear "Tubby" Hayes and Stan Tracey. Being a raucous character, Bill was soon thrown out by my spinster sister landladies, who also objected to his paying in "Scotch" money; I followed soon after, having been accused of blowing up the heating boiler.

I immediately visited a Piccadilly lettings agency, which eventually offered a mutually acceptable pitch in Weymouth Street, just a step from Oxford Street. Marylebone was then an archetypal "London village" with a high street to match. Elizabeth David, writing in her column in *The Spectator*, cited one of its two greengrocers as "the best in London". Just round the corner in Paddington Street was a fishmonger invariably featuring a massive Dover Sole, decorated with assorted shellfish in its widow.

The flat was a top maisonette sublet by a couple of chemists whose main clients were international horse-racing organisations, which required drug-testing services. Our living quarters were comprised of half a dozen rooms, occupied by five tenants, all public school except me. (This was just before the era of "mixed" flats). Turnover was reasonably brisk, as people moved on to jobs outside London, got married and so on. "Newbies" were selected by interview, with the main criterion being "would they fit in?" One of the many subsequent interviews involved an older man than ourselves. He had worked in New York and introduced us to the new concept of "gay" (this was 1963). He was not invited to join us. According to Graham Hodson (who later acted as my best man and became another lifelong friend) – and I honestly cannot recall this – I scored by putting forward a theory of sexual selection where women were classed as those you had bedded, those who had been rejected (e.g. they were unattractive, they lived next door), and those who were highly desirable but unattainable e.g. Princess Margaret. This was, of course, a galaxy away from "Me-too".

One of my flatmates suffered an embolism and was taken to the nearby Middlesex Hospital. He was out, fit and well afterwards and actually married one of the nurses. We obviously got to know staff during our visits, and I was invited to join the hospital rugby club (I had been playing indifferently at No.8 since I was 11, culminating in a 70-nil defeat against Oriel College when playing for HQ BAOR). What sprang out of this was a sort of club, which could have been named "New Build Climb". As usual, London was being developed and reconstructed; our challenge was to climb each tall building just before it was topped-out. The Post Office Tower was next to the hospital and was our first ascent. Later on, the new Park Lane Hilton was our target; we were amazed when we reached the top to be asked to put on ties! (I made that bit up, but when we all went up to use the real rooftop bar – yes, we had the Ritz treatment). Mention of that area of Mayfair reminded me of a very 1960s experience when I was limbo-dancing at Les Ambassadeurs, after which I accompanied my friend Felicity, a model, to her house in Cadogan Square in a horse-drawn carriage – those were the days.

Two of my flatmates were members of the Honourable Artillery Company, the oldest regiment in the British Army, which is still active in Afghanistan and other theatres. One of the great occasions for the HAC (apart from the Lord Mayor's Procession in the city) are the Summer and Winter Balls held at its HQ Armoury House in the City of London. White tie and tails or military dress uniform were compulsory for these occasions and strict rules enforced. I took my partner into the Suttling Room, an all-male bar, for a dare, only to be told by the Regimental Sergeant Major that I must leave immediately. Today, invited by member friends, the protocols are much more in line with current mores.

During the Profumo Affair, Christine Keeler had a flat in Devonshire Street, a few yards from our flat. We used to chat with the paparazzi grouped round her doorstep of an evening; they regaled us with stories of an old local man who had hired prostitutes to tie him naked to a radiator in his flat and proceed to urinate on him. Another close resident was Stephen Ward, who lived in Wimpole Mews, next to our local, the "Dover Castle".

Marylebone was the home of many "celebs", a term unknown at the time and which denigrates the breed, in my view. Kenneth Williams, wearing a high-collared Italian shower-coat, could be seen in Paddington Street, looking neither to left or to right, followed by his mother. At the Baker Street end, Cliff Richard could be seen sitting in the window of the "Two Bays" sandwich bar. In the High Street, Peter Sellers was often seen driving his Rolls-Royce towards Mayfair. Again in Marylebone High Street, I was lucky enough to see the Beatles dashing around in black suits, filming *A Hard*

Day's Night in front of an Indian restaurant with a turbaned Alfie Bass as its door-keeper. Virtually no one else saw this happening, as I recall. The location is now a bank.

Jeremy Lewis, sadly a late flatmate, a "blue button" in a city stockbroker and son of Jay Lewis, the film director (*The Baby and the Battleship*, *A home of your own*), invited Liz and I to the Shepherd's Bush Theatre to see *The Frost Report*. Afterwards, we met John Cleese and Graham Chapman and, with Jeremy, had a meal together in an Earl's Court Italian. John had just returned from the States and confessed to disliking smutty humour; this certainly characterised his outputs latterly.

Humour was always part of the atmosphere in the flat. Our telephone was connected to the "Hunter" exchange and the number was very similar to that of the nearby Planetarium, and we quite often received enquiries from would-be punters. I usually told them that due to heavy cloud over London, there was no vision. As young, party-going men, we tried to make the best of swinging (or, as some said, "swingeing") London. For example, one of my acquaintances organised a party on the Embankment, with two pantechnicons parked back-to-back to form a dance-floor. Talking of that part of London, two other flatmates decided to buy a barge, moored at Chelsea Harbour. Liz and I were invited for supper and thoroughly enjoyed the nautical atmosphere in the fine old boat. Unfortunately, sometime later, when the tide receded a tad too much, the hull was stove in by a delinquent oil drum. Their response was to have a new barge built – if only they had bought a house in nearby Fulham at that time. Marylebone was a quiet area at weekends, due to the predominance of offices (this meant invitations to the Home County family homes of my flatmates, of course, which was very kind and pleasant). Otherwise, most of the parties were held farther west, in Chelsea and Kensington. Being also keen on the visual arts, I visited the Tate Gallery (now Tate Britain) regularly; my first and most impressive view was of Francis Bacon's first retrospective in 1962, and seeing his triptych of figures at a crucifixion and the "Screaming Popes", based on Velasquez. An architect acquaintance who accompanied me and knew of my admiration for surrealist artists like Max Ernst and Rene Magritte invented a character called Max Bacon, just to underline his Philistine tastes.

Liz, my wife to be, lived in a flat in Chesham Street, Belgravia, owned by a well-known osteopath. Quite by chance, one of the Johns in my flat was going out with one of Liz's flatmates. On the way back to Chesham Street, I dumped my escort in Gunter Grove and we proceeded to her flat. Here I was introduced to Jane Elizabeth Lloyd Davies from Neath, South Wales. She worked for Van den Bergh, a subsidiary of Unilever, on the Stork Margarine Account. Working at Sainsbury at the time, she and I had something in common. We started going out together, but it was a bit of a miracle that it lasted. I was invariably late for dates and was developing into the classic "unreliable boyfriend". However, after over 40 years of marriage and three children, she changed me radically, for the good.

The character makeover struck me many years later. I was teaching an accounting class in South London, when a mature student, a woman of about 60, remarked that, as a lecturer, I was a "perfectionist" and that

I must be a Gemini. After the class, I was intrigued and asked her to explain, particularly as I was a Piscean. She hooted with laughter: "They're all over the place!" I had to admit that Liz was a Gemini. Although privately I have little faith in the predictive power of the Signs of the Zodiac, the actual outcome was undisputed, whatever the chemistry involved. We then agreed, with further reference to her own successful marriage relationship, that partners can have a major effect on each other over the years.

To reel back the years, I had become unofficially engaged to Liz at a party my ex-flatmate, Mike Drewery, hosted at his and his wife's place in Battersea. Standing in front of the fireplace, I suggested that we holiday together in Scotland. We drove up to Pitlochry in my Sainsbury Mini. The next evening, we saw *The Amorous Prawn* at the local Repertory Theatre. Things went well and I later met her parents and siblings in Wales. We were married at The Forward Movement Church in Neath, South Wales, on 26 March 1966. The reception was held at the Dragon Hotel, Swansea, and the honeymoon spent at Cala d'Or, Majorca. The hotel faced a tiny but idyllic beach, with friendly British expats in the bar. When we revisited it two or three years later, there were several hotels, and the once quiet beach was packed with holidaymakers. The next year, we took our first child to Ibiza. When I was settling James in his cot, I was bitten by a mouse. When I finally found the manager to complain, he just offered me a large Osborne brandy. Fortunately, this did the trick. However, James nearly fell out of a window, the beach was covered in oil from a ship spill and the general standard of service was poor. At just under £70 per adult, the tour company gave us a full refund.

We had started married life in a brand-new town house in Orpington in Kent. Liz had a job with the Potato Marketing Board, somewhat similar to the one she had with Unilever. She promoted the board by giving cooking demonstrations to local London branches of organisations like the Women's Institute. One obvious problem we both faced, particularly as we were both working, was the absence of a telephone. On enquiry, I was told that waiting time for an installation would be up to six months. Seeking the advice of friends, the best that came up was: "Get on the waiting list, pronto!"

The next day, I walked over Blackfriars Bridge from my office at Sainsbury headquarters to New Bridge Street Post Office. There I wrote out a telegram to the then Postmaster General, Anthony Wedgwood Benn, explaining that I was a businessman in urgent need of a telephone. "You'll be lucky," remarked the clerk as he read it. Three days later, the red telephone I had ordered was installed. Of course, this kind of problem does not arise in the era of 5G.

We had an immediate circle of friends, particularly Nick and Sally Nicholson. Sally had worked with Liz at Van den Bergh, and this meant a name change for the latter because the company already employed two Lizzes. The result was that the family and half of our friends called her Liz and the other half Jane, her first name. I had to keep remembering this for ever. We met up at the Rose & Crown at Halstead. Three or four of us joined Sevenoaks RFC and also formed the Octagon Golfing Society, which survived into the 21st century with frequent trips to local clubs and to French and Spanish courses.

Then a sudden major upheaval – I moved back to Edinburgh with my family. I was very familiar with Scotland and joined a company that needed some help (discussed in the Retailing chapter). The rewards were: a new challenge, much wider and significant experience and a substantial uplift in seniority and salary. The only problem, as I came to realise, was my wife.

We had little problem in selling the house; it was just two years into a 99-year lease. Just as we had agreed a price with the civil servant who, with his family, was keen to buy the house, he suddenly asked for a £200 reduction. When I demurred slightly, he burst into tears in front of his family as we stood in the open-plan first floor. As I was about to take up a job paying more than twice my current salary, and my new employer had promised to pay all the removal costs, I happily agreed.

We bought a four-bedroom detached Wimpey house in Swanston Avenue in the south of Edinburgh. From the bottom of the garden, uninterrupted fields stretched to the Pentland Hills – a brilliant view. Since then, the new city ring road has been built, along with a plethora of new houses. I was delighted to be back in the country where I had spent 20 years, but Liz was less sure. She loved Kent and missed her many friends there. Of course, over the next three years, we welcomed them for stays with us and visited them in return. Contact with Liz's parents was maintained, which was particularly important because when Simon was born, they had two grandchildren to see. We flew to Cardiff to stay with them, from Edinburgh, Glasgow or Newcastle, depending on flight availability. We usually drove to Manchester to visit my parents.

We began a Sunday habit, maintained for many years, of driving out for tea, notably at the Peebles Hydro, 20 or so miles south of the capital. Here, James and Simon could run around the spacious hotel lounge and outside in the big park-like garden. We tried to start up the regime of dinner parties, which we had begun after our marriage. I invited various colleagues from work for dinner. In one case, Liz had provided gazpacho for the first course and the guest, a junior manager, complained that it was cold. There were one or two good restaurants in the city, although today it is a positive cornucopia in that regard. We particularly liked going out with special friends, like the Sharps, to Prestonfield House with its oval dining room and peacocks in its lovely gardens.

We did not make many friends in Edinburgh. Most of those we did become friendly with were from Glasgow, the United States and England. I adored Edinburgh and was thoroughly enjoying my job, but Liz did not share my enthusiasm. Familiar local phrases to mirror this attitude are "East Windy, West Endy" or "When you go to a home in Glasgow, they put on the kettle; when you go to one in Edinburgh, they put on Netflix."

As Liz became more and more miserable with life in the city, particularly as it was so far from her family and from those she regarded as her real friends, I began applying for jobs back in London. Unfortunately, a long national postal strike had begun in 1971. Being now well embedded in the retail sector as a careerist, I had the wheeze of sending "on spec" letters, directed through the internal communication systems of targeted retailers. Eventually, I secured a consultancy post with Allied Shoe Repairs, based in Croydon. This involved a new house search in the West Kent area, where most of our friends lived. Finally, I found a five-bedroom semi-detached house in Westerham. Clearly, Liz needed to be won over. She organised three or four of her friends in the locality to inspect it – and they were unanimous in their approval. We signed up to the deal and moved in around August 1971. I had put our furniture in storage in Edinburgh and, as it happened, took an inventory. The pantechnicon bringing the furniture south was cut up by a Jaguar on the A1 at Duns – all effects were written off. A few days later, one of the removal men appeared with a garden fork in one hand and a cuddly toy in the other – all that was salvaged, he told me. It was lucky that we were staying with our great friends, the Scobles, at the time. The inventory came in handy for our insurance claim.

B.A. Cox, Mary, David, Winifred Cox

Roger, left, in BAOR

Liz

Steph

Simon, Roger, James

Roger in WADS farce

Chapter 7

OISTREHAM

The Barony of Oistreham was given by conqueror William the First to Eustace of Boulogne, husband of Edward the Confessor's daughter. That was in medieval times, and we have dropped the Norman French to call it Westerham. This small town is just on the Kent side of the Surrey-Kent border.

Our house is at the end of a private lane, which no one has seemingly claimed ownership of. The four original houses were built around 1908. The story is that a local builder decided to develop some ground adjacent to the parish church; apparently, there was an economic recession at the time, and pre-empting the ideas of John Maynard Keynes, they decided to create income through investment when costs were low.

As one would expect, when we took up residence, the neighbours were quite different from those of today. Living next door was David Martin, who immediately introduced us to the most popular local, "The Old House at Home". The landlord was Ernie Dumbleton, a real character – an ex-Thames Lighterman who hailed from the Borough. David was one of the first to import degraded jeans from the US (this was in 1971). Out of the original five pubs in the town, only one now exists (one, like London Bridge, was exported to the US); by the same token, the six petrol stations have been reduced to one. When we arrived in the town, a gallon of petrol cost 3/9 (18 pence).

Liz, once we had settled in the house and to life in Westerham, decided to apply her culinary skills in a business, which eventually became "Leave-it-to-Us", and has its own website. I had always wanted Liz to write a cookery book. Eventually, *Finger and Fork Food* was published by Marks & Spencer and was a great success. She also collaborated with Josceline Dimbleby in her book. Again, Liz appeared on BBC Television in a series on female entrepreneurs.

I was always very enthusiastic about the venture, even thinking we could turn our large drawing room into a restaurant; the lack of car parking space put the kybosh on this idea. However, on numerous occasions, we turned it into a dining room for parties for friends, seating up to 30. Over the years, male friends have created dining "clubs" where we meet for lunch or supper in various pubs. Again, our love of fine dining means that we visited rated London restaurants with special couples with similar tastes. With a wide set of friends, parties were being thrown all the time in the 1980s and 1990s. One celebrating the 50th anniversary of VE Day was held in a friend's mansion in Kent, and we were asked to appear in the costumes of the time. A swaggering group of SS officers draped themselves over the sweeping staircase, accompanied by a uniformed "Hitler maiden" who was actually German and who cried out: "If only my father could see me now!" Nick Nicholson was dressed as Henry Hall, and I was a senior British staff officer (my wife Liz told me that several woman had fallen for me, but I never found out who they were). Another gathering involved dressing up as punks – I wore a punk wig and managed to squeeze into my eldest son's leathers.

We were very lucky to have, at the top of our lane, a small junior school. All three of our children attended and enjoyed a very sound basic education. Croft Hall School was run by Mrs Wilkinson, who I chatted to in our Market Square while writing this.

Between the Market Square and our house used to stand the old Westerham Hall. David Bowie had one of his early concerts there. According to locals, the audience was somewhat scanty, but there was one reminiscence. David had dinner at the upscale Marquis de Montcalm restaurant next to Quebec House, the home of General Wolfe, who defeated the former on the Heights of Abraham. Anyway, Bowie queried the bill and allegedly refused to pay. Mr Zarb, the proprietor, locked the rock-star in the restaurant until he settled up.

Westerham Hall, before it was demolished to make way for houses, was the venue for productions by the Westerham Amateur Dramatic Society (formed 1921). All of the five members of the family appeared in plays such as Mortimer's *A Voyage Round My Father* and Thomas's *Under Milk Wood*. Apart from these classics, I enjoyed playing the barrister in the former's *The Dock Brief* and the telephone engineer in Neil Simon's *Barefoot in the Park*. Arthur Pratt will long be remembered as the concert hall chairman who came up with "Traffic in the town is steadily increasing, and one man is being knocked down every day – and he's getting pretty fed up with it!" and "Anyone from outside the town?" – "Yeah, I'm f'm

Biggin Hill!" yelled someone. "Well, you'll feel a jolly sight worse before we've finished!" was Arthur's response to the obvious plant. My own childish instincts emerged as an audience member when I could shout "You Rotter!" when the pantomime villain declared his dastardly intentions.

Stephanie (always known as Steph) was born in Sevenoaks Hospital on Boxing Day 1973. By the time she was three years old, Liz decided that, as her business was booming, she needed some in-house help. We contacted an agency that provided us with the first of three au pairs. The first girl was Swiss and, sadly, she lasted barely a week. Not only was she very untidy, but one day she was on the phone to her boyfriend in Switzerland to find that he was in bed with another woman. She tantrummed and booked the first flight back home. The agency apologised, offered us a refund and provided a substitute, Lilo, also Swiss; temperamentally, she was much more acceptable, with a sunny disposition. However, when the family was holidaying in Cornwall, she deserted us to join the boys on the beach we were on at Rock. Eventually, these natural traits cancelled out her skills as an au pair and she also had to go. Finally, the agency sent us Chelo, a Spanish girl, who was perfect and later moved on to help other friends with their offspring. When we were on holiday the next year near Barcelona, her father, who was a Valencia-based pottery manufacturer, invited us to lunch. This was at Vinaroz, halfway between the cities, in a glass restaurant on the beach. The main course was made up of over a dozen shellfish, including razorshells, washed down with "Freixenet".

Steph left Combe Bank School and became a secretary in supply-chain management and in specialist recruitment.

She earned her spurs in the former, a Moroccan-owned produce importer with major clients. She became involved in a dispute between Sainsbury buyers and the supplier but managed to talk the former into retaining its connection. Unfortunately, her job was terminated when the firm, located in the former Sevenoaks Library, went into liquidation. She spent some years as a nanny and working in kindergarten in Kent, possessing a natural affinity with young children. She instantly won a job at a Tonbridge school by immediately kneeling to greet a child there, demonstrating the "X" factor, according to the headmistress. Today she runs the catering business founded by her mother over 50 years ago. Her first marriage was dissolved. She married Matthew Jenkins and they have a son, Max, who is at school in Oxted.

Most Saturdays I used to take the three children swimming. We enjoyed travelling to a variety of pools from Orpington, Sevenoaks, Tunbridge Wells and, occasionally, the Olympic-sized facility at Crystal Palace. The boys enjoyed the delights of the Imperial War Museum and visiting computer game shops in Soho. Sundays involved tea-room visits that we had started in Edinburgh.

The males in the family were all great Monty Python fans, and I was determined to see *The Life of Brian* when the film was first released. James and a friend, plus Simon and myself, drove up to a cinema in Lower Regent Street. The film was licenced for showing to 14-year-olds and above. James and his friend were of legal age, but Si was only 12. An attendant gave him a suspicious look as we entered, but we quickly seated ourselves together. We all enjoyed the rather naughty film, except Simon who confessed much later that he was constantly looking round for possible ejection. James was a great David Bowie fan, and a few months later, I drove him and his friend to Milton Keynes Bowl to see and hear the great man. We all saw him at Wembley in one of his last concerts.

Simon Cox was born on 8 November 1970 and was educated in Sevenoaks. As mentioned previously, the whole family were involved in local dramatics and he was no exception. After a time in publishing and retailing, he decided on acting and spent a foundation year at Kilburn College, where we saw him in his first Pinter, *Mountain Language*. He began studies at the Drama Centre, Chalk Farm, in the mid-1990s; previous alumni include two James Bonds, Anthony Hopkins and Frances de la Tour. Russell Brand was also in Simon's group. Among the plays we saw him in at the Centre was *A Chaste Maid in Cheapside* by Thomas Middleton. After graduating, he toured both Germany and Italy, presenting classic playlets in English to schools, somewhat similar to the many *Horrible Histories* he played in, subsequently around England. He has twice toured Faulks' *Birdsong* around Britain and been in runs of shows such as *The Thirty-Nine Steps* in London theatres. Both Simon and I have been long-term admirers of Harold Pinter and over the past years have managed to see about two-thirds of his oeuvre in London theatres.

As with many actors today, there have been fallow periods. Early on, Simon took up executive chauffeuring in Mercedes "S" types. One of his passengers was Robert Altman, the director who remarked that in Hollywood most "real actors" rested as waiters. He punctuated this wisdom, according to Si, with a substantial fart as he got out. On another occasion, his task was to drive the Prime

Minister of Malaysia around London over the period of a state visit – the challenge was coping with a tight motorcycle escort on each occasion. He also drove the model Claudia Schiffer and her boyfriend, but more interestingly, another famous model, Naomi Campbell, had to be driven to an airport. When he arrived, Simon was directed to an executive jet parked on a stand. Minutes later, a large convoy of SUVs drew up and out of the second stepped former president, Clinton. He strode up to Simon, shook him by the hand and thanked him for bringing "Miss Campbell" to the airplane they were to fly together to the United States.

Back at "real work", Simon has been in two films – one, *Going off Big Time*, Liz, Steph and I watched in a Croydon cinema, along with four other people, two of whom walked out. The other film went straight to DVD. His TV commercial work, on the other hand, has figured clients as diverse as Microsoft, the WWF, Esso, Virgin and Cadbury, as well as a Greek lager and a German Supermarket, both filmed abroad. Incidentally, he was forced to abandon his surname and could not adopt his middle name of Andrew because other Equity members had already appropriated them. So he has borrowed one of his brother's, itself handed down from his maternal grandfather – Lloyd. Simon also helps his sister with catering supplies, including a bar at functions, if required.

James Cox was born in Bromley on St George's Day, 1968. He lived in Bromley with his second wife, Phillipa, an actress who also works for Lime Studios. He was educated in Sevenoaks and was the only one to attend university – Roehampton – where he earned a BTEC. He joined the Ministry of Defence as a clerk, followed by a spell at HMV in Bromley, where he gained an encyclopedic knowledge of current music. A key career change occurred when he was recruited by Sevenoaks Council Rates Department. Having learned enough about Council Tax, he moved on to the tough London Borough of Newham, in the East End. Here he plunged into the more interesting (i.e. difficult) world of Business Rates. A taciturn man, in time, he became expert in pleading the Council's court applications for the payment of rate arrears in the Borough. This was probably instrumental in his subsequent employment by Wandsworth Borough Business Rates Department; this London Borough is known for charging some of the lowest rates in Britain. Running a small department, James continued developing his career through further higher level experience and the gaining of more professional qualifications. Recently, some much-needed rationalisation has occurred with the merging of rates services in Wandsworth with those in adjacent Richmond. This was further complicated by a policy decision to move the outsourcing of rate collection to an internal system. This has clearly changed James's job radically. On top of that, the Covid-19 pandemic has precipitated an avalanche of CVAs, where businesses such as retailers – some of them very large – have petitioned for bankruptcy proceedings and thus rates relief. He confessed that this was very testing, but as someone who chairs meetings of London Borough business rates managers at County Hall, he is adequately armed. He and his wife have now moved to Whitstable, the lovely town on the North Kent coast.

Liz and her siblings, Nicholas and Joanna were born to Rhysted Lloyd and Margaret Davies (nee Arnold).

All three of the children attended private schools. Liz was particularly keen on sport and represented the Welsh Girls' Schools Hockey Team at Wembley as goal-keeper. Their grandfather was the Reverend R.R. Davies, a well-known Welsh cleric, who preached at the Forward Movement Hall, Neath, where Liz and I were married. R.R. Davies was called to the First Presbyterian Church, The Heights, Wilkes-Barre, Pennsylvania in 1914 and the family emigrated. They returned to Wales in 1919, but moved back in January 1921. His task was to help found a new Westminster Church, a replacement for an old building founded in 1843. The new church was dedicated in 1924. R.R. Davies was awarded a Doctorate in Divinity by Lafayette College. The family moved back to Neath in 1926 and finally comprised of five children: Rhystyd, Gerald, Robert, Alan and Megan.

The family did not talk much about these far-off days, although Alan and his eldest son had visited the church and parts of the Midwest. I became fascinated with what I heard, however, and began a lifelong interest – indeed, admiration – for the United States. Our extensive travels there our described later in this chapter.

As mentioned, living just 20 miles from London, we have spent quite a bit of leisure time there, invariably driving up if possible. Personally, I'm not too keen on public transport, although it is good to have excellent transport links to and from the centre. I always think that the place is slightly unsettling for young ones, so I used to try to soften the image by calling it "London-Bundon" when driving the kids up. Silly old Dad.

No such subterfuge when one day in late 1990, I took Liz up to Leicester Square to see Pauline Collins in the film *Shirley Valentine*. I had just bought a white Volkswagen Golf and as I drove up, the news came through on the car radio that a demonstration over the poll tax was due. All was reasonably quiet as I parked in Charing Cross Road. We then walked to Leicester Square to see the film. When we re-entered the road, it was filled with people and police, some on horseback. Liz had had a couple of hip operations and was on crutches. We popped into a nearby café, which was filled with others "sheltering" from the mob. After about half an hour, we decided to try to reach the car. A large American limousine had been overturned in the middle of Charing Cross Road; standing on it was a wild-looking young man waving a large banner. Beirut?

When we finally reached our car, it was the only vehicle of a dozen or so that had not been turned over. The rear passenger window had been broken by a brick, which was lying on the back seat. Apart from that, the vehicle was undamaged, possibly because there was a disabled card behind the windscreen. We then managed to turn the car round and drive it to the Strand, avoiding Trafalgar Square, which was the epicentre of the riot. My son James gleefully took the brick as a trophy to display in his bedroom.

On a lighter note, a year or two later, I was driving eastward along South Lambeth Road when we were stopped by lights at Vauxhall Cross. A crowd of "squeegee merchants" rushed out to our vehicle and set about "cleaning" our windscreen. I adopted the usual expressionless face and looked straight ahead, while Liz exclaimed, "Well, at least it keeps them off the street!"

This chapter, you will have gathered, is about our family, which started on 26 March 1966. I believe that it has been largely a success. This has been due mainly to one person – Liz, my wife. In an uncomplicated way, she liked everyone and, as usual in normal human relationships, people liked her. This is not to say that she lacked guile. For example, when being interviewed by a prospective client, she would ask: "Have you any thoughts on your main course?" If this was something "off the card" like Squabs St Hubert, she would smile sweetly with her rejoinder: "What a delightful idea, but have you thought of…" It usually worked.

One important strand in our family life has been travel. So, without apology, the rest of this chapter is devoted to our love of the big wide world. Liz brought friends to us, and without these we wouldn't have had so many holidays. But she was selective. Tales of "Delhi Belly" put her off India. One of my students, a Muscovite offered us a flat in the capital, with use of a Mercedes – no to repressive regimes. "South Africa and its lovely Garden Route, darling?" – no to violence in Joburg etc. I tended, on balance, to agree – why tempt providence with the memory of Edinburgh?

In any case, the world is a big place. James has been to Thailand, Steph has been to Alaska, Simon has been to Romania – neither I nor Liz have been to these places. Liz liked Southern Europe, the Caribbean and the United States – again, our tastes were identical.

We were fortunate in our first family trips abroad to stay with friends who had villas. In 1972, we stayed with the Mackays in Kifissia, a suburb of Athens, where you were taken round the kitchen before your meal in a restaurant, and if you were a millisecond late in driving away from lights, you suffered a massive blast from dozens of car horns. The next year, we were with the

Nicholsons in Malta, where after a first encounter with shark fin, we discussed its possible importation to Britain. In 1975, we decided to share a villa at Begur on the Costa Brava with our friends, the Breens. The plan was that our wives and the two youngest children of each family would fly to Girona, and Mike and I would drive the 1,000 miles or so with the two eldest children and an au pair, in my Maxi. On the way on the autoroute, we ran out of petrol. Almost immediately, a CRS (riot police) van stopped. They were charming and offered to bring us petrol from the next service area. It later appeared that the tourist ministry had ordered the police to be friendlier to foreign tourists.

Later on, we stopped at a large campsite and pitched our large tent. That night, we experienced the most horrendous rainstorm and the tent was devastated. Fortunately, there was just enough space for our passengers, and Mike and I slept in the car. After suffering the camp loos, we enjoyed a French breakfast and managed to reach our destination late that day to link up with Kate and Liz and the other four children. The holiday was great fun, the only problem being that I lost my car keys on the beach at Tamariu; we managed to have the ignition key changed to restart the car. Fortunately, I had arranged AA cover, which also included a full set of hoses (I thought) and other pieces of kit for emergencies.

On the drive back, we avoided the A7 in France (following the tourist bureau suggestions of the time to see more of France). Moving up a fairly steep incline on an extremely hot day, one of the radiator hoses burst, losing most of the coolant. We got the children, Louise and James along with Heather into what shade there was at the side of the road and lifted the bonnet to inspect the damage. The first problem was that, stupidly, we had no spare water, and second, the AA kit did not contain a hose that would fit in a Maxi engine compartment. As the children were out of the way, in desperation, I urinated into the radiator in a vain effort to rehydrate the system. We were in trouble.

Suddenly, the Cavalry! A Mark 1 Cortina drew up and a slim, moustached young man leapt out. Apparently, he worked for Ford and supplied us with a useable hose and enough water to replenish the radiator. He refused any compensation, and we thanked him profusely. We reloaded and started off. At the top of the hill, about 200 metres from our stop, was a huge Total station.

My desire to go to the United States was met in 1988. Initially, I went to see friends who lived just north of Chicago. Derek Norman, who I had met in the Army, had married a German girl, Urzel, and they lived with their three children in Highland Park, Illinois. First, I flew to New York with Virgin, landing at Newark, New Jersey. My first impression was how clean the airport was. I stayed at the local Holiday Inn. With memories of my stock market experience (see next chapter), I was keen to see Wall Street. Finding myself in Columbus Circle eating ham on rye, I asked a police officer how far away the financial centre was – "83 blocks" was the laconic response. I took the subway.

I flew American Airlines to Chicago around midday. The flight was packed with business people off to meetings in the city. Dressed smart-casual, and the last to board, I attracted a shout of "backpacker!" as I searched for a seat. Lunch offered beef, chicken and vegetarian on a two-hour flight. Today you would be lucky to be offered a pack of peanuts. Derek met me at O'Hare Airport, and I enjoyed a few days of German-American hospitality and seeing the architectural splendour of this fascinating city. While I was there, I spent some time on researching for an article on US retailing for a British journal, using the spacious facilities of the Kinzie Street Library. Next day, I took a hire car to Milwaukee, Wisconsin. At that time, many cities presented videos about themselves – in this case reflecting the ethnic mix and the beer heritage of the city. On the way, I was hit by Hurricane Arthur. The day before, I had seen a weather forecast on TV that went over six scenarios as to how it could affect Chicagoland, as the locals call it. It was preceded by actual shots of Chicagoans boarding a plane in the Caribbean to escape the storm – "It was terrible" said one. The rain, which I finally encountered on Interstate 94 made it feel like I was driving on the bottom of a swimming pool. I had to pull over and stop for several minutes – it was the worst downfall I had ever seen.

In 1992, I took Liz to Chicago to see the Normans. We flew United (the local airline) direct to Chicago with a British crew, who were magnificent. At that time, the Normans lived with their three children in a spacious wooden summer-house in Highland Park on the edge of Lake Michigan. Chicagoans had these as second homes to get away from the city. Unfortunately, these attractive houses are being replaced by big square dwellings that look like small hotels. The same is happening in Britain in towns like Beaconsfield, particularly in high-end areas like Burke's Road.

Liz loved Chicago. You could travel by double-decker trains through towns like Winnetka and

Evanston to the River Chicago, where you could sail on a commuter ferry to other parts of the city centre. A feature on the street were old London buses for tourist sightseeing. Skyscrapers range from the almost gothic Wrigley Building to the Hancock Tower on the famous Michigan Avenue with its superb shops. I think Liz had been fired up by my liking for America – and the Normans – and so my plan now was to try to travel there every five years, and so 1997 scored.

As Liz had not seen New York, we decided that because we were planning a complicated trip to America, we would "bundle up" several elements of it. It seemed logical to start on the East Coast. When we landed at JFK, the scene was reminiscent of a Third World country; there was triple parking in front of the arrivals and the weather was really tropical. I gazed despairingly around for a sign of some form of transport to Manhattan. Almost immediately, some form of transport appeared in the shape of an elderly stretch limousine parked some way away on a piece of churned-up land that resembled a building site. The dishevelled man beckoned us to join him and his mate in the vehicle. Summoning up my naivest view of humanity in what was clearly a tough position, I smiled weakly to Liz, and we carried our bags to the Cadillac and sat in one of the rear seats; facing us was a six-inch screen TV. There was not much conversation from the front, but our "guide" did point out the Shea Stadium and the USTA Tennis Courts on the way. When we reached the Novotel, we were charged $100 (going rate at the time being $60). I suppose the extra could be classed a risk premium – but for whom? Anyway, the short stay in the city was a tonic, being together as sightseers. We went up the Empire State

Building and the old World Trade Centre, of course. In the evening, we went "off-Broadway" to see *Five guys Named Moe*. Next day, we flew to Chicago on a Delta flight from the inner-city La Guardia Airport. Again, we enjoyed a great time with the Normans (who came to stay with us in Kent a few months later).

The original idea of seeing Liz's grandfather's church had still not been realised, so in 1997, we decided to do just that. I had written to the minister, the Reverend Deming, to explain our interest but received no reply. After an interval, I also wrote to the mayor of Wilkes-Barre, again pointing out our importance as descendants of a previous incumbent of one of his local churches. Within days, a letter from the mayor arrived, acknowledging our interest and welcoming us to the town (more tourists!); by the same postal delivery was a letter from the church, saying it was all right to come. Success! When we arrived in Wilkes-Barre from staying again with the Normans, flying from Chicago via Cincinnati, we booked into a motel with a Red Indian totem pole, on the banks of the Susquehanna River.

To be charitable to the Westminster Church, the tardiness of the reply may have been due to the fact that our requested Sunday for a visit coincided with a ceremony where the choir was to wear their new uniform. Whatever the problem, we were courteously greeted by the Reverend Deming, who showed us a photographic portrait of R.R. Davies that was hanging among others in the church. We attended the service, and afterwards we had lunch with members of the congregation. Over burgers and fries, we chatted with a lady who claimed to have "walked out" with Liz's father as a teenager. Afterwards, we were driven round the city by a local doctor, who was a member of the congregation. He told us the story that the Susquehanna (a tributary of the mighty Mississippi) had flooded so badly in 1974 that hundreds of caskets had floated out of the cemetery. And that was it. American friends were surprised at the somewhat muted reception we had received "so soon after the untimely death of Princess Diana". Another story! Diana's sad demise had occurred on the weekend before we were due to fly to New York. When we heard the startling, if not entirely unexpected news, Liz wanted to cancel the trip. Well, you can imagine the quandary. I did say, well, Chicago is a well-connected city and we just might see a telecast of the funeral. Sure enough, Channel 4, Chicago's finest, provided a complete programme – at 3am local time. Liz said afterwards that it was kind of funny with American voices and interpretations. But her holiday was not completely spoilt, although the Americans we spoke to mostly said "What the heck are you doing here, now?" In fact, she walked right past the condolences signature station under the Wrigley Building.

We did use our time in Pennsylvania to do some touring. I hired a Dodge Saloon to drive to Hazelton, an old mining town south of Wilkes-Barre: we saw a film of Lithuanian immigrant miners – and the Welsh – happily cracking on at the coalface. Later we saw the Gettysburg site and I drove through a truck lane at Harrisburg, costing me $10. Clearly, in that part of East Pennsylvania, we had to visit the Amish country. This was filled with souvenir shops and a marvellous statue of a miner in the middle of Lancaster. Then we got hopelessly lost, almost touching the suburbs of West

Philadelphia before I remembered to turn left to Reading and on the interstate past Bethlehem and on to Wilkes-Barre.

I had messed up the return flight to Chicago, and a rectification would cost $600. So we hired a Toyota at the Wilkes-Barre/ Scranton Airport. Hertz allocated me a Wisconsin-plated vehicle, clearly for their own convenience. We set off on Interstate 80, the only transcontinental motorway in the US, apart from the 90, which plies north and south. Being a great driver, Liz did most of the steering, and the statutory 60 limit was often breached. In Ohio, she overtook a Suzuki Jeep filled with young girls. Shortly afterwards, an old black Cadillac crossed over the central reservation from the east-bound carriageway; it contained a load of men wearing black fedoras, who ignored us but stopped the girls. I could only think that this was an incident that was being filmed. So, being a romantic, I thought "Yes, this is the Midwest and it's just normal." Liz told me not to be stupid. Then we stopped at Youngstown for a snack at McDonald's. We were not aware at the time that the city was well-known for crime.

When we reached Gary, Indiana, I decided to telephone the hotel in Chicago we had booked into. Liz and I took turns to work out how to use the phone until beaten. She asked a woman who had just emerged from a McDonald's; the woman started screaming at her while appearing to protect her son, who she obviously thought was in danger. We quickly retreated and drove off. At the time, Gary was the leading murder city in the US. Finally arriving in Chicago, we stopped the car in a run-down section of the city, just off the freeway. Then Liz spotted a couple of men loitering on the sidewalk.

Having driven in Chicago during previous visits, I had a good idea how to approach the centre, so I took over. The hotel was just off the "Golden Mile", just behind the Hancock Building. It was, in fact, a converted nurses' hostel, and we were offered the penthouse suite. That evening we went to a "gay" restaurant, recommended by the hotel; it played local "garage" soundtracks. We rounded off the evening at a performance of *Chicago* at a nearby theatre. Next day, we returned the car and boarded our 777 at O'Hare Airport. The flight had been overbooked, and we were offered $600 and a room at an airport hotel to be "bumped". Unfortunately, I had to be at work in Greenwich the next day.

One social feature of this particular time was that many of our friends had children who were being married abroad. Our next trip involved a wedding in New Zealand, so we decided to turn this into a round the world holiday. Trailfinders planned the complete trip for us – a very competent service. We flew to Hong Kong and found other friends at check-in who were bound for a resort in Malaysia. After seeing the usual sights in this fascinating port, we all flew to Sydney on a QANTAS flight. On the way, I chatted to a Scotsman who claimed that this was his 33rd trip to Australia. I guessed he was now paying less than half the nominal fare he paid for his first flight. Sydney is not as exotic as Hong-Kong, but it bursts with "Digger" power. When we toured the famous Circular Quay where the cruise ships and the didgeridoo players congregate, who should we see but John Major, the former UK prime minister, smiling broadly at us and here for the cricket; he was accompanied by his wife, who looked less elated.

Having said goodbye to our friends, the Simpsons, we flew to Christchurch and stayed in the Crowne Plaza IHG Hotel, filled with South Korean guests. We visited the cathedral, which, subsequently, was badly damaged by an earthquake. At supper, in a very pleasant restaurant, I tasted fresh tuna for the first time. It was quite bloody. The wedding was held in Ashburton, a town south of Christchurch with its main street dominated by agricultural machine distributors. This was apposite, because the bridegroom was a farmer's son and an engineer on a large yacht. Our hosts were the Roberts, who ran a farm near Bala, North Wales. Quite a few mutual friends had made the trip, and the wedding was a great success. The next day, we went on a trip to Mount Cook. On the way, the guide gave a fascinating description of the various irrigation systems on the farms we passed on the huge Canterbury Plain. It tied in well with my geographical knowledge, but Liz remarked that it was too much like Wales and went to sleep.

We took a shuttle flight to Auckland and boarded a double-aisle airliner for our journey to Los Angeles. It seemed to me that travelling back to Blighty the same way, via Singapore, missed the point: crossing the International Date Line. Neither of us had visited the West Coast before (my only regret was that we were missing an exhibition of Derek Norman's paintings in London). We stayed at the Roosevelt Hotel on Hollywood Boulevard, which had a replica of Charlie Chaplin sitting on a bench in the foyer. Just opposite was the Oscars theatre, which had pillars in it, each with the years of future ceremonies on them – American optimism that came true well into the 21st century. Our trip to Universal Studios was an eye-opener, with the town hall set for *Back to the Future*, among many other exhibits reminding one of other great movies. We shared a taxi with a couple from up-state to tour Beverley Hills. This was spoilt, not only with the driver's commentary being marred by a guttural European accent, but devoid of any useful let alone interesting information on the many stars' houses we were passing. It reminded me, oddly, of a horse-drawn ride round Central Park we had made seven years previously. Irish coach drivers come over for this work in the summer, and this garrulous man told us of a group of Californian tourists. When he pointed out the Dakota Building, which overlooks the park, and told them of the shooting of John Lennon, they did not appear to have heard of him. Ending our "Tinseltown" tour on a "celeb" note, we dined at The Ivy next to Ozzy Osbourne and his family, still wearing the neck brace after his unfortunate fight with his quad bike.

At airport check-in, we were sharply dealt with by a steely-eyed Russian woman. Liz's case was searched to reveal the iPods we had searched the World for – the kids were grateful. We had to remember that the rather gruff treatment was occurring only three years after 9/11. Back in the air, on our way to London, we thanked Uncle Robert for the bequest he allowed us after his passing, for our trip of a lifetime.

The next year, we were invited to a wedding in Buenos Aires. One of Jim and Sue Brown's two sons, who travelled widely and was a fluent Italian speaker, had met an Argentinian lawyer, proposed to her and been accepted. We stayed at the Claridge Hotel in Buenos Aires, and as Argentina was still suffering from its debt default, prices were relatively low – the

Government had made the risky decision to peg the peso to the US dollar (this reminded me of a stay during the 1990s in Famagusta, North Cyprus, when the Turkish lire collapsed, paying for our hotel bar bills and snacks). The wedding was a grand affair in another luxury hotel, with a huge room devoted to ice cream, as part of the wedding breakfast. There was tango dancing by top stars of the art and a Beatles tribute band – all very professional. We had visited an estancia, with the offer of horses for those with equestrian leanings. We all attended the world final of the international polo championship, and some of us men visited the La Boca with its colourful houses and had a walk round the famous football club ground. Liz and I also went to the Perón mausoleum at Recoleta and, of course, we all enjoyed the thick, thick slices of Argentinian beef in the city restaurants, a place that reputedly has the widest boulevard in the world. Two less admirable features of the city at that time that I noticed were the standard use of civilian gate-keepers outside most shops (not the US meet & greet "my name is Jack" merchants) and the awful condition of all the many taxis we used.

Friends' offspring weddings abroad continued in 2008. James Breen, one of the sons of our local dentist, had taken a degree in philosophy at Bristol and had entered the TV industry. He was soon involved with the early "reality" show *Pop Idol*, precursor of *The X-Factor*. Any incipient talent in demonstrating dog tricks to singing ballads would be revealed. The story has it that the floor manager should intervene if a contestant showed signs of "cracking up". Young James, as producer, would have none of this and ordered that the cameras be kept rolling, whatever happened (within reason). The perception was that viewers generally approved this as part of the reality. US talent scouts noted this, and James was invited to go to LA to help launch the American version of *Idol*.

Simon, our second son, was to be the best man at the wedding, where James was to marry a British girl. The marriage ceremony was held in a church in Pasadena, a pleasant town north of Los Angeles. Guests were greeted after the service by the traditional mariachi band as they made their way to the reception in Altadena a nearby suburb. There was a hope that Simon Cowell would appear, but he did not. I had a dance with Cat Deeley, who was well-known in US TV dance circles. She is a Brummie, so we chatted about the joys of Sutton Park. There was a slightly embarrassing pause as Liz and I joined our designated round table for the wedding breakfast. We faced eight young men, friends of James, whose expressions were somewhat devoid of friendly gaze. Liz, always poised in this sort of situation, immediately addressed one of them: "John, when are you going to move that rubbish you've left in our garage?" Immediate glacier melt.

As we were in California again, we decided to visit San Francisco. We shared the driving of the SUV up Route 1, a very scenic but tortuous road which follows the Pacific Coast. Our first night was spent in the university town of San Luis Obispo, at a stop that was on the site of the very first motel. At dinner, the waiter introduced himself and elaborated on the menu, for example: "Soup or salad?" Simon immediately responded: "I'll have the super-salad, what's in it?" Our next stop was in the lovely town of Monterey, staying in the plush Plaza. On the way, we stopped to go round

Hearst Castle, the press mogul's old home. This contains many artefacts from the old Hollywood years – and a large indoor swimming pool (incidentally, Steph's husband Matt works for the Hearst Corporation in London as an advertising designer for titles such as *Elle* and *Red*).

Arriving in San Francisco, we booked into our hotel in the Tenderloin district, which is less than a mile up the hill from Union Square. Guidebooks noted the relative sleaziness of the area, but the hotel was friendly and comfortable. The first thing I planned to do was to take us to the top of the Bank of America tower, which has a bar and a stunning view over the city. This was a popular move and set up the mood for our visit. That evening, we attended a performance of Neil Simon's *Speed the Plow*, about shenanigans in Hollywood. Afterwards, we had a few drinks in an Irish bar. Here Simon phoned Steph, who, although it was early morning in Kent, carried out a jolly conversation with us for an hour. Next day, we were ferried across to Alcatraz and met one of its last convicts, who was selling copies of his memoirs, which stressed the fact that no escapee was known to have successfully reached the city, through the vicious currents in the channel.

Over the past 10 years, Tenderloin and some other parts of central San Francisco have further declined socially. This has been due to the pressure on rents, overcrowding, homelessness and unemployment, all leading to increased poverty. The huge success of the tech companies has been a major cause. A 2018 article in *The Economist* painted a dark picture of this, even including a map of street defecations in the city and its surrounds, to starkly illustrate the dire situation.

Back to weddings: European venues included Estremoz in Portugal (the Edelmanns), Waterloo in Belgium (the Haywards), Lourmarin in Provence (the Reeds) and many more in England, Scotland and Wales. A surprising number of weddings involved family repeats – in one case where six siblings were happily married off.

As suggested previously, Liz was particularly fond of the sun. In Mauritius, we stayed at a hotel that was being run by a captain and flight attendants from Sabena, the Belgian airline that had recently collapsed. Although the hotel was comfortable, pleasant and an asset in the beautiful island, Liz, being a Cordon Bleu trained chef, was unhappy with the standard of the dishes produced by the largely Indian cooks. This led to a flaming row with the management. In spite of this, we enjoyed our stay. The same could not be said of the Seychelles the next year. The hotel we had booked into was to be demolished and replaced. The bar area, for example, was poorly designed, with a very restricted view of the beach. When we were shown to our room, I gave the porter $2 as a *pourboire*. For the next hour or so, a trail of staff appeared at our door bringing food, drink, beach towels and other unbidden items, obviously in expectation of more hard currency. This was faintly amusing, but when we had landed, I was surprised to see an Aeroflot aircraft parked. That evening, we descended to a basement bar that had been taken over by a group of very noisy Russians – both aircrew and tourists. Although the Island's beaches and the capital, Victoria, were pleasant and acceptable, this holiday was possibly the worst we had had together.

We both decided that the Caribbean was preferable to the Indian Ocean (but in mitigation of the latter, it must be said that flying Air France there, which we did, was wonderful, with good service and the best cuisine of any carrier I have used). Our favourite island was St Lucia, which we visited three or four times – Barbados about the same number. On one trip, we went on a submarine trip from Bridgetown, with a captain called "Les from Luton", who rather caught Liz's eye. Part of his schtick was to go through a safety routine before we sailed: this was carried out with great gravity, until he burst out laughing, and told us that it was all fake, and with over 1,000 submersions there had never been an accident. We survived. One year, we decided to try the Sandals resort on Antigua – "The island with 365 beaches" – which was the one and only "inclusive" holiday we ever had. There were several glass-bottom boats for hire, and we went out with a group of scuba divers. Someone had thrown a piece of bread into the water, which attracted a shoal of Barbudan chub. The fascinating thing was they all queued up for their single bite, giving way to the next fish. When disembarking, we mistimed it and were deposited in a big roller, dishevelling both of us. Security guards initially barred us from entering the hotel because they thought we were free-riders.

In 2009, Liz enjoyed three holidays. We were both fond of the Italian lakes, she particularly Como, where we stayed in one of the several five-star hotels. Later on, we flew to St Lucia with the Simpsons and, last of all, Liz went off to a hotel in South West Majorca with Stephanie – she stayed there most years with her sister Joanna, friend Sally or even me. In this case, it had just been renovated and was even more delightful for her.

When she was back at home, she complained of back pains. After a preliminary examination, our GP told her to rest and arranged an appointment with Guy's Hospital on a Monday. The day before, she came down from her bedroom and asked for some of the chicken Steph had cooked. Eating alone in the dining room, we heard her make a sound – she was having a stroke. An ambulance was summoned to take her to "The Prue" (formerly Farnborough Hospital in Bromley). She was soon transferred to King's College Hospital in Camberwell. This is an incredibly busy place, at any time. The staff were clearly under enormous pressure, and the noise level was very high. After a couple days of this, Liz asked to go back to her original hospital. This meant that a 20-mile trek into Central London was cut to less than 10 for us. She was diagnosed as a case of pancreatic cancer, which had spread to liver, lungs and the bile duct. She died in the evening on 23 December 2009. Her funeral was conducted at Tunbridge Wells Crematorium at 12 noon on Wednesday 6 January 2010. A memorial service was held the next day in Westerham Parish Church. The church was very full, in spite of a heavy snow fall. Mourners had travelled by road from places as far away as Elgin in Morayshire (our dear, close friends, the Hayward family). Tributes were given by her brother Nick and by Sally Nicholson, while the reading "She is gone" was read by Gill Hayward. Tea was supposed to be served in Crockham Village Hall, but snow up on the downs was so deep it was virtually cut off. Fortunately, a children's party at Westerham Hall was cancelled, so it was only a short walk through the churchyard to the hall, where a marvellous collection of photographs, many of which I had not seen, illustrated many events in her busy life. Some people object to two things about modern funerals: pictures of the deceased on the front of the order of service and the singing of popular, modern songs. Liz's picture shows her in radiant form at one of the Mackay's weddings, and the record of *One Day More* brought tears to more than my eyes. She would have loved it and recognised that it was a heartfelt tribute from the many who had been privileged to have known her.

James was married to Phillipa Sarll on 26 November 2011 at West Heath in Sevenoaks. This venue was originally the school Princess Diana last attended.

Stephanie was married to Matthew Jenkins on 9 February 2013 at a mansion house venue near Marlborough. They now have a son, Max, who has had this book dedicated to him.

Simon lives with his partner Wendy Davis in Worthing, yards from the sea.

I mention my children again now, because I realise how lucky I am to have three healthy, bright and gorgeous offspring – and their partners (and Maximillian) – although they are now in their 40s and 50s. Fortunately, I am able to see them regularly and share in their lifestyles and success. Linking up with old friends is great as well, in pubs, restaurants, country walks and the like; as is making new friends, which I did as a volunteer for the National Trust, and supporting other charities such as the Royal British Legion, the NSPCC, Education Support, and those dealing with cancer, particularly of the pancreatic variant.

Feeling very depressed, I decided to take a short break after Liz's passing. I had never been to the Grenadines, and my only thought on the island archipelago was the drink that the children liked, mixed with soda, when we were holidaying in the Mediterranean. I first flew to Barbados and was transferred to an "island hopper", a high-wing, single engine plane that is commonly used in the Caribbean. It can seat about 10 passengers, and all seats were filled on my flight. After leaving St Vincent, we landed on Bequia, where almost all the passengers disembarked. Perhaps I was disoriented after eight hours flying, or had had too many piña coladas, but I followed them. When the aircraft took off, and I had no luggage, I knew I had made a bit of a boo-boo. I quickly booked into a hotel and telephoned Palm Island, my planned destination to say that I had been delayed. Next morning, I was covered in mosquito bites – served me right – and I checked into the next flight. An hour or so later, we landed on Union Island, described as the Island's southern transport hub by the guide book. It was actually the smallest airport I had ever landed in, but it was sweet because I found my case standing in splendid isolation in the middle of the little terminal. The hotel launch was ready to take me across the short trip to Palm Island, and there on the jetty was a waiter with a large chilled glass of mixed fruit juices. A good start. On the flight, I had noticed a woman, apparently on her own, but lost her when the flight landed. Later on as I was sitting down for dinner, I noticed her standing in the queue. I quickly went over and asked if she would like to join me; she seemed glad to be rescued. She was a tall Scottish woman, around 30, who had trained as an architect, but tiring of the work, had joined a large US design company at their Hong Kong office. Now she had another new career (like me?).

A keen sailor, she had had her little sailing yacht brought to and moored at the hotel. It was named *Pink Lady* and her plan was to sail her to Antigua in the Northern Leeward Islands (mentioned elsewhere in the holiday section). Then, in partnership with a local hotel, she would offer trips and sailing lessons for tourists; she would be supported by a small team of equally attractive girls dressed in pink, the colour of the yacht. During the northern winter, she would operate in the Caribbean, a ferociously popular sailing region, and in the Summer at Martha's Vineyard on the Southern Massachusetts coast. We had dinner each evening together, became friends and ended in a tearful farewell. She seemed a splendid, outgoing woman, who was hopefully starting on her third career. Best of luck, Kirstie.

First of all, I tried singles tours, not for any specific reason except the sheer joy of travel and "being there". With the tour operator Just You, I visited Rome and Central European capitals and, finally, took the Route 66 tour in the US. Oddly, I objected to the presence of already partnered couples, just a few, but it seemed a negation of the whole idea of "singleship". I switched to Newmarket as a tour operator, which provided me with the best cost-effective holiday in the US I have had so far (but the Route 66 tour was magnificent for its sweep of that great country).

In late Summer 2016, I began a journey on what is variously referred to, even today, as "the main street of America" or, more logically, "The Mother Road". Its offspring today is Interstate 80, and it is difficult to find a trace of it in Rand McNally. We started in Chicago, with a sparse breakfast in the Hancock Tower, which Uncle Alan had climbed during its construction in 1974.

In the evening, we all went to Buddy Guy's big music club. Next day, we left Illinois for St Louis, 300 miles away. Our tour guide and coach driver both claimed to be Vietnam "vets", and we were informed that the local pronunciation of the state was "Missoura". When an explanation of US retail payment systems was outlined, it became clear to me (and on many occasions) that a simple signing at payment was the vogue, and that in general, "chip and pin" was not used. This was obvious at the Memorial Arch shopping mall, when I tried to pay for a sweater for my new grandson with an Amex card, using one of those old sliding card machines with a carbon printout. Incidentally, the hotel was located in an industrial section of the city, and the bedrooms were filthy; unsurprisingly, the staff messed up our room allocations. Three of us grabbed a taxi and enjoyed a few drinks in a central bar, although we were pre-warned. This before the Ferguson riots. Next day, after touring the city, we visited Branson in the evening. This is one of the many music-based cities in the country, and we watched a great cowboy-themed show of song and dance. We were all given masses of different lapel pins here as memoirs – a very Southern US cultural trait.

On to a Springfield motel, somewhat unimpressive. We were invigorated, however, by a rally of American veteran automobiles in its car park; this provided an antidote to the continuous boredom of American food. Drinks were fine. Next day, we entered Kansas for a few short miles, before hitting Oklahoma City. The National Memorial for the victims of the bomb placed by the so-called US "Patriot" movement was the first stop. It is contained in a beautiful park with 168 chairs, each one commemorating a victim. We then crossed into Texas through the "Panhandle" in its north. The Glen Campbell CD that started playing was quickly moderated as we drove through Amarillo, as some tour members decided to hum "that song". The next stop was in New Mexico, at an Albuquerque Hyatt. American hotel breakfasts can be the best meal of the day, especially if you get in early; they may even be part of the package. You can have a sort of bacon, egg and sausage in many places, but it is not British. The best eggs are hard-boiled, and some hotels provide passable porridge. Yoghurts are plentiful, and fruit drinks are acceptable. But not coffee. That day, we tripped to Santa Fe, the state capital, and visited the Capitol. After that, we discovered a brilliant "museum of the West" filled with cowboys and Indians and all things binding them together. The city is very attractive and surrounded by stunning countryside of mountains and deserts.

On the way into Arizona, there is a statue of Glenn Frey in Winslow, his birthplace. The Eagles single, *Take it Easy* was written about the town. Like many places on the Route, there is always a souvenir shop, much of it taken up with reminders of 66 itself. This helps to mitigate the obvious poverty of many parts of the South. The Route, in a sense, is their local industry, relying on the hopefully increasing international – as well as home grown – interest in it and its history. Our next overnight stop was in Flagstaff, and next day, Nevada and Las Vegas, of course. But not necessarily – Route 66 does not run through the city, and a female passenger, who was on her second time on the Route, said that it was not on her previous itinerary. Anyway – the "Sin City". Walking down the Strip, I found it a bit of a curiosity. Entering the Bellagio, I looked for signs of its namesake, the gorgeous Lake Como village I loved. How naive! Actually, I was searching for a bar at 11am and a waitress came out of one and asked me if I was looking for a job. I said no, just a beer. Eventually, I got one, for free, and sat alone in the gambling den. Of course, I knew that there were no clocks, but on trying to exit, I discovered that these places are designed to make them difficult to leave. When you manage that, possibly sloshed, you are on a high walk with shops, leading to the next casino. Later on, the Grand Canyon was a marvellous, relatively uncomplicated sight.

Next day, we reached the end of the road in Santa Monica, on the Pacific coast. The tour guide claimed to have helped set up the signs marking the end of Route 66. We were taken on a tour of Los Angeles, naturally focusing on Hollywood, notably the culturally opaque Chinese Theatre, the stars' pavement marks and, something new for me, a big new gift store called La La Land.

After a night in a Burbank hotel, we boarded the coach for the last time, to take us to the airport. There had been over 40 people on the tour – large by most standards for this kind of trip and, as usual, a preponderance of women. It had been a wonderful and most interesting trip, sentiments I evinced when I was asked to thank the guide and driver for their services. It had been a trip of over 3,000 miles and had gone without any real problems. I emphasised this in heartfelt thanks to the two men, on behalf of the group. The Vietnam veteran guide wept a little, and everyone seemed happy. Just You had recommended a tip of $20 per day for each man, and I guess that it was nearer $10.

The next year, I had decided to change my tour operator to the more conventional Newmarket Group. Possibly as a result, this was the second-best US tour I have experienced. It was well priced in spite of my being a single and was surcharged. My tactical aim here was to cover as much of the south-eastern states as possible. Flying into Atlanta, we immediately made for Montgomery, the Alabama home of Rosa Parks and her statue. The hotel was part of a disused railroad station, next to a small shopping mall that contained several Mexican restaurants – a cuisine I was unfamiliar with. The meal I had was a signal for more to come. Next day, when we passed Mobile, we were in Louisiana. The country we were driving over in our coach was generally flat, like much of the South, and highly agricultural; land devoted largely to cotton, but also tobacco and cereal production. New Orleans was the next stop, where we stayed for two nights. The parades and the jazz clubs in the French Quarter, which still has the atmosphere of the 18th century, were unmissable. We toured the city by bus, seeing the plantation area whose mansions, built for the Cotton Kings, made Beverley Hills look like a council estate. On the second day, I decided to escape the tyranny of standard American food and had lunch at the Ritz-Carlton. It was excellent and I gave the pretty waitress $5 – and stole her pen. I would rank it as my third favourite US city after Chicago and San Francisco. On our way to our next stay at Lake Charles, still in Louisiana, we visited Baton Rouge and toured the State Capitol (administrative centre).

At another stop, we inspected a plantation house where we toured the slave quarters, which were obviously replacements for the originals. A carpenter in the group remarked that the design of the joints in the huts suggested very recent construction. Chatty but informed notes on the life of the inhabitants and laudatory descriptions of the last chief slave – a woman – provided a sympathetic commentary. Inside the house itself, female guides and attendants were dressed in historic costumes. I was at the head of our group, and I was suddenly faced by a small, severe-looking woman, who addressed me: "Where y' from?"

"London... Well, actually Westerham, where Churchill used to live."

"Mr Churchill – what a wonderful man! Did you see his statue in Noo Orlins?"

"Yes," I lied.

"Where y' goin' next?"

"Houston."

"Houston – that's an oil town!" she hooted.

"Well, there is the Space Center."

"Ye-e-s," she conceded, doubtfully.

I decided to tease her: "Then, after Texas, we go into Arkansas, to Hope." (The home of the Clintons).

"He's no friend of mine!" she exploded.

Attempting to re-rail the conversation, I said: "Well, then we go onto Tennessee."

"Nashville! Are you goin' to the Bluebird Café?" she shouted, somewhat rhetorically, ending the conversation. I thanked her and we moved on. Several couples behind me seemed to have appreciated this spontaneous bit of knockabout and one, from Wales was particularly enamoured; we stuck together for the holiday and we still exchange Christmas cards.

Houston turned out to be a solid but typical American city, rated the fourth biggest. Its fast growth has necessitated the concreting over of a vast flat area covered in houses. It becomes badly flooded after storm surges and as a port. In the centre, near a wooded area, is what can only be described as a panoramic sculpture of a huge cattle round-up. In typical PC style, the cowboys are, in terms of ethnicity, white, black and yellow. Little Richard was an early resident before he found fame in Motown. The Space Center was much as expected, except that some of the original control decks and equipment was also on show. The next stop was San Antonio, a delightful city with a river running through; this was lined with walkways on both banks, with a big range of restaurants and bars – the latter including a British pub run by expatriates. We stayed in the old Crockett Hotel, which faces what is left of the Alamo battleground, now overbuilt with urban sprawl. Davy Crockett, a hunter turned politician, was killed defending against the Indians and is commemorated in a popular song.

After two days, we turned north to see a great deal more of Texas. We had a break at Waco, and I suggested half-seriously if we could see the site of the cult-based massacre that had occurred there a few years before. I was given short thrift on this one, but I had been arguing with our guide since the start over details on aspects of the United States. He was British and an ex-Army sergeant. As an infantryman in the Greenjackets, he had poo-pooed my Corps experience as a National Serviceman. However, it was mostly banter, and we got on well, generally. At Austin, another fine but fast-growing city, we were invited into the Capitol building, the third one I have been to, so far. These, of course, are legislatures that make laws for their state within the Federal structure of the US. Normally, you are shown the assembly area and given loads of stuff explaining and lauding their state.

North to Fort Worth, where we were booked into a Hyatt. Twice a day, there is the attraction of a cattle run outside, attended by cowboys in traditional garb. We were all given scarlet neckerchiefs, advertising the city and the event (I wore it in Waitrose as a mask during Covid-19 and so frightened an elderly lady that I have not touched it since). I found out that the city is the home of American Airlines. Next day, Dallas, which forms a conurbation with Fort Worth, Arlington and other areas. The big attraction here, of course, is the JFK exhibition, on the site of the assassination of President Kennedy in 1963. While I found it interesting enough, most of the information was well known. This is where fake news scores – the last section was devoted to the conspiracy theories. Moving on to Texarkana on the state line, we entered Arkansas, the birthplace of Walmart and, as mentioned, the late home of the Clinton family, a modest house for a future president, whose records are to be found in Little Rock; a state capital that saw much turbulence during the initial fight for racial equality in the 1960s. Now to the last state on the tour, Tennessee. Two cities are the focus of visits, both known for popular music. The first, Memphis, is obviously best associated with Elvis Presley. We stayed in the Guest House Hotel, opposite Graceland. Incongruously, Presley's private aircraft are parked in front of his old house, which is a relatively small and unimpressive mansion; one or two members of our group were scornful of the furnishings, largely on the question of taste. Memphis itself contains a department store that hosts a daily duck walk for the children; the ducks end up in a fountain in the middle of the ground floor. Much more interesting is the Sun Studio where Presley and many other singers recorded their hits. B.B. King has a restaurant named after him at the top of Main Street, above famous Beale Street. The second, Nashville, is much more revered, particularly music lovers with a wider view of popular music. We visited Studio B, which is on a crossroads flanked by three other studios, marking out the city as the epicentre of American music, even if we take Detroit into account. However, the talk we were given in Studio B about its history and significance was lack-lustre and devoid of audio or visual illustration. We also wanted at least to see The Grand Ole Opry, but it was booked for months ahead.

Our last break before climbing the Blue Ridge Mountains to Georgia was in Chattanooga, where we saw a replica of the famous "Choo-choo". It was interesting, from a railway enthusiast's point of view, that there were several parts of the tour where real locomotives were lovingly preserved in their natural habitats of rails and wagons. Now that trucks move materials and produce around, the South is particularly bereft of any signs of Amtrak. Then we boarded our flight from Atlanta to Heathrow.

The next year (2018), I filled out another part of the States by travelling (again with Newmarket) from Virginia to Massachusetts. Initially we flew to Washington and coached to Williamsburg, then from here we visited Jamestown, an early British settlement. The museum there was filled with artefacts reflecting the foundation of the colony in the early 17th century. When preparing for the trip, I found an article in *The Telegraph* that told of a headless skeleton, preserved in Virginia, which was thought by the researchers who had found the remains of Richard III to be a titled Londoner who had crossed to Virginia to revive the settlement from certain extinction. Our tour guide, an American, knew nothing of this and gratefully took the cutting from me. In my experience of tour guides, they are sometimes poorly informed (I am reminded of a guide in Austria, in Haydn's birthplace, pronouncing the composer's name phonetically, while virtually the whole coach was shouting it correctly). In Williamsburg, most of the tourist guides were dressed in early costumes. One academic gentleman, similarly attired, perorated in a grand period house of the tussles with the British as they were slowly driven out of their erstwhile possession; my know-all reminder to him that all this occurred on mentally-ill George III's watch was summarily dismissed. This was America, after all.

The next day, we drove west to Charlottesville. This was the city involved in the new and growing current political disturbances. BLM supporters had gathered to petition the removal of a statue of General Lee, a Confederate leader in the civil war; they were opposed by right-wingers, one of whom drove a car against a member of the former group. Our guide briefly mentioned this. Later, we gained some fresh air, when we reached the ridge of the Appalachian Trail on our way north to Washington. I was amazed to find, when we arrived, that the Smithsonian institute occupied over a dozen buildings in the city, but we had no time to enter any of them. We managed to see the usual sights – the White House, the Lincoln Memorial, the Federal Capitol, Arlington Military Cemetery – and photograph them among the huge crowd of tourists milling around. Fortunately, the weather had been beautiful, so far.

It was more interesting for me to travel this highly urban part of the East Coast. For instance, I had not realised how close Baltimore (home of *The Wire*) was to Washington, and that Interstate 95 passes through Philadelphia as one hits New Jersey at Trenton. The built-up area goes on implacably up to Paterson in the north of the state, where we were staying in a Holiday Inn. Next morning, going down to my usual very early breakfast (who wants to miss a minute in this fantastic country?), I found the place crowded with truckers, muttering about "Nebraska", "plazas" (toll-gates) and the like. That day, I made my third visit to New York, and we were blessed with a young, enthusiastic and well-informed guide. The coach took us through Harlem, which I was unfamiliar with. Having been up the 104-floor Trade Centre 10 years before its terrible demise, I found the replacement buildings most impressive, and as 21st century towers, an improvement.

Off to Boston. My aim in touring America is certainly not to visit every state, but this trip certainly added substantially to my score. This trip we travelled through New York, Connecticut, Rhode Island and Massachusetts (before, on this journey – Virginia and Maryland, just skirting tiny Delaware – maybe to be visited in the future, to research its mysterious corporate registration industry). In Massachusetts, we stayed in a very pleasant seaside hotel in Hull, on the southside of Boston Bay. In the morning, I boarded an early ferry, filled with besuited commuters, to do a quick inspection of the city and some shopping for presents. Next day, we enjoyed a guided tour of Boston, covering mostly the Italian section of the city and the harbour, which contains various US historic naval ships. When I asked about the famous Irish element (which had brought in the Kennedy family and other famous contributors to this great country), the guide replied that we just didn't have the time to go to "Southie". As consolation, I found a cosy bar near the harbour that served the most delicious scallops, washed down by classic Boston craft. Back to London from Boston Logan.

The next planned trip to the States is to attend my nephew Andy's marriage to Kaitlin at Hauppauge, Long Island. I received a card saying "ok covid, new plan", putting it back three months – but I'm still looking forward to my ninth trip to the great country.

As listed in the Chapter Contents this memoir first describes the life my family and I have experienced, to date, and the last five chapters describe the various parts of my work career and how they hang together.

Chapter 8

RETAILING

Like all industries, retail distribution has been subject to change. Of the six retail businesses I worked for between 1960 and 1975, only one remains in its original form – J. Sainsbury. The lessons absorbed with them helped me to learn through doing, and this experience provided the material for five books.

LITTLEWOODS

This large, privately-owned firm was a combination of three businesses – a football pools enterprise, a mail-order company and a retail variety chain. I was hired as a trainee manager of the latter when I was demobilised from the Army in 1960. Based in Liverpool and founded by the Moores family, which later gave their name to the city's second university. The stores division competed with other variety chains in shopping centres all over Britain, notably Marks & Spencer and British Home Stores. I was initially posted to the Edinburgh branch, and training started with our being allocated three or four product sections, under an experienced female supervisor. One of our duties was to check new products and pricing in our product areas in the local M&S. Our training was thorough, both in store and at head office in Liverpool. One week, I was posted to Dumbarton on the west coast to be deputy manager there. Awakening in my hotel on the first morning, I found myself locked in with no one at all in the premises; I had to break my way out to go and open the store.

My one regret was that, while in Liverpool and regularly visiting the Hacienda Club, we never saw the Beatles, who made regular appearances there. It turned out that they were in Hamburg at that time. The best part of the Littlewoods experience for me was that it provided solid grounding in retail practice. I felt that I had been a modest success as a trainee, although the manager did say that I would do better in supermarkets. Mr May later became head of a southern group – and I joined Sainsbury. In the event, I only lasted a year with Littlewoods; the final straw was that I was found with my then girlfriend in a store cupboard, an event only compounded by my landlady coming to the store to complain to my boss about my conduct in her house. As my family had just moved to Manchester, I was homeless. Fortunately, I was rescued by mates who rented a large communal flat. These events, and the thought of working in "Wee Scotland" for ever, suggested a move south – to the Great Wen (which actually means "big boil").

THE NATIONAL CASH REGISTER COMPANY

Although NCR was not a retailer, my post as assistant marketing research manager gave me an important insight into the retail environment. As the main supplier, at the time of cash registers to British retailers, my primary task was to advise potential customers on the key problem initially facing them; as hotelier Conrad Hilton put it – location, location, location. Although customers such as Marks & Spencer and Sainsbury bought hundreds of machines, big retailers employed their own site assessors. I was to deal with independent and small multiple retailers, which still provided plenty of work; essentially, a sales promotion activity. This entailed a great deal of travel by public transport – I was never offered a company car. The job included the investigation of the proposed shop's catchment area, the competition, the local demography, accessibility, footfall and the overall size in terms of household spend in the area of influence. I became acquainted with the mostly American research into retail siting, notably Reilly's law of retail gravitation.

In the course of the work, I had many trips to Ireland, both North and South. On one occasion, I was driving to Heathrow in my own Morris Minor, when it broke down on the A4. Abandoning it for a taxi, I just missed my BEA flight to Dublin and had to board an Aer Lingus Viscount. Unfortunately, the only seat available was first class. So I was forced to eat the "Golden Shamrock" breakfast, complete with champagne. On arrival, I was met by the chief salesman and immediately driven to the general manager's home in Dalkey. There, I spent most of the day drinking Jamesons and listening to the two yarning about their country and their work. The sales chief took me to my hotel, and the next day, I began researching a new shopping mall in the south of the city. When I returned to the office in London, a memo had been sent out reminding us that only NCR directors could fly first class. It is always useful for a manager to maintain good relations with subordinates. My boss, Gordon Blackall, was a tall, amiable man who had been working in East Africa. General research was part of the remit of our department, and we had both been involved in a study of London hairdressing salons. The company's market share in this sector was low due to the incursion of fashionable Swedish registers, as well as those produced by a Brighton-based firm. The survey's aim was to assess the current situation and future growth trends in this segment. The finished report would be sent to a wide group of company management, including those at NCR head office in Dayton, Ohio. There were some government statistics on market growth over the past five years (the sort of data I helped produce for the Census of Distribution, later at British Bakeries). My main task here was to interview the owners of hairdressing salons in the central part and in the "four quadrants" of London.

The final section of the report showed a table of the past trends and future projections of cash values of the British hairdressing market (the Government Blue Book had suggested a steady average of 5 per cent inflation). Gordon had given the final draft to the secretary, who not only had typed it but had duplicated a hundred copies. By this time, Gordon had gone on holiday, leaving distribution to me. Unfortunately, the crucial conclusion showed the preceding years' sales building up to around £90 million in 1965, while the estimate for 1966 was given as £10 million. There was clearly no way that this report, with its laughable conclusion, could go out to the NCR constituency. The immediate messenger would be symbolically shot, and Gordon and the department would be in the firing line. So I told the secretary not to worry but to type out a hundred little scarlet-coloured sticky labels with the correct figure and cover up the offending number. My thinking was simple, in that the wrong number would disappear, but the importance of the forecast would be highlighted.

Of course, when Gordon returned, he was very grateful. The real point was that if I hadn't liked the guy, I might have just let it go. I re-met Gordon in 1970 when we were both on a Laing-sponsored trip to Paris to view the "ring-centres" and enjoyed a typical three-hour French business lunch. Lunch at head office in Marylebone Road was often spent in the Allsopp Arms next door. In 1962, all the managers were dark-suited, and we youngsters obviously followed this trend, often accompanied with collarless white shirts; this meant wearing celluloid collars, attached by studs, something that harked back to Edwardian or even Victorian times. I had inherited this style from my father's ministerial roles. As a result, I had my collars cleaned and starched by Collars Ltd, whose brown cardboard containers were delivered to me in Hampstead. The area around the office was very residential, with many blocks of residential flats; these housed many older women – widows, spinsters, divorcees – who used to come into the pub, apparently to view the potential talent (us). They were invariably dressed like figures in a Beryl Cook cartoon, in long black coats and small hats, tightly pinned to their hair. Their predatory style suggested that they were scanning for boys of the toy variety, but neither I nor any of my drinking companions were ever propositioned. We avoided David Bowie's mistake when he was emerging from HMV in Oxford Street, and he caught the eye of a fan.

One of the little-known links between NCR and its clients was based on the versatility of its little silver Class 100 stand-alone cash registers. In the old days, NCR sales teams allegedly used guerrilla-style sales tactics with independent shopkeepers; they would rush into a shop and plonk down a machine on the unsuspecting shopkeeper's counter, accompanying this with a brisk, pointed sale spiel. This approach was reckoned to create sensational sales volumes. A sort of reverse action occurred when I was working at Littlewoods in Edinburgh; a couple of thieves rushed into the store and lifted a Class 100 off the leading counter and disappeared into Princes Street!

J. SAINSBURY

In those days, the jobs column of *The Daily Telegraph* provided the possibility of an improved career with a famous retail name. At this time, the company was opening stores of around 10,000–15,000 sq. ft., similar to the size that Aldi and Lidl are launching today. In 1966, Sainsbury passed the £100 million sales level and led UK supermarkets in turnover until Tesco overtook it in the mid-1990s. I was interviewed at head office near Waterloo for an hour by the personnel manager and later met my new boss for 10 minutes. This was the perfect proportion, I felt, for good interviewing practice. Sainsbury provided a two-week induction course for "junior officials", which covered all aspects of the business operations, from interviewing staff for the pie factory over the street to the slaughtering of pigs (and, horribly, of rabbits). I never experienced such an intensive process anywhere else, but it was a significant investment and an inculcator of loyalty, in my view.

My new job was the assessment of projected Sainsbury supermarkets, which, naturally, involved much travel, for which I was allocated an Austin Mini. The process used in researching and reporting on a site was based on one that I had devised at NCR, with additional support from colleagues and databases available in the company. There was also a growing literature published by government and private sources. As at NCR, I relied on a team of two clerks for delegated support. That was probably the easy bit. Reporting also included a presentation to a board committee chaired by Lord Sainsbury himself, dressed in the grey alpaca jacket that all store managers at that time wore. Directors used to approach me informally, from time to time, to ask whether such and such a town might be a good place for a store. I tended to oblige them with a response, if I happened to be in that area, but in 1966, even in the South of England, it was always a "no". However, time tells – Otford (Sevenoaks) being a stunning example. On another occasion, Timothy Sainsbury asked me to write a report on the projected population of Britain in 2000. I duly went over Waterloo Bridge where the Registrar General's office was situated in the Strand. After chats with various statisticians, and a riffle through some documents, the general estimate was 73 million. As we now know, this forecast was around 25 per cent out. It only showed how true complaints are about how difficult it is to produce accurate estimates of future conditions. In this case, the relative unknowns were the impact of the contraceptive pill and the serious inflation of the 1970s, which cut real incomes, helping to force more women into work, all conspiring to reduce family sizes.

Sainsbury was, in many ways, an exceptional employer. There were nine economists in the firm charged with overseeing meat products, site location and so on. This compared with only about 20 economists in the Treasury, I believe. My colleague, another Roger, the meat economist, told me that the new Aston, Birmingham, branch (recommended by my predecessor in the post) had doubled its sale of pork pies on the second day of opening. "What's the score?" I asked. "Two" was the answer. It has to be explained that at that time there were multitudes of little cooked meat shops in the city, a difficult number to factor into an investment decision of this nature. Again, Catford in South East London looked like a growing shopping destination. But when M&S moved out, it was clear that Catford had been severely downgraded, sitting between Lewisham and Bromley, each with brand-new shopping malls. Both of the above Sainsbury stores had to be shut down, sadly.

I had married in March 1966 while still with Sainsbury, and my section, in a very practical Sainsbury way, had given us an ironing board as a wedding present. I decided we needed more cash, with a new house and a prospective family. Like many well-managed family companies that offered satisfying work and an attractive career path, pay was moderate. I resigned with great regret. The company and I could have parted earlier, if a certain incident had gone the wrong way. My flatmate, Mike Drewery, who was a space salesman for the art magazine *Apollo*, invited me for lunch at El Vino's, where the mythical *Private Eye* journalist Lunchtime O'Booze hung out. In line with city wine bar menus, which had tiny food listings and massive wine sections, we must have consumed three bottles of Malmsey between us. Mike offered to drive me back to my office in his Mini, so we tore over Blackfriars Bridge at insane speed, and I managed to stagger back up the steep stairs at Stamford Street. My ultimate boss, the trading director, looked me up and down and declaimed what I supposed to be the penultimate admonition: "You are not a real Sainsbury Man!" I was then given permission to go home.

I had asked the trading director to act as one of my referees, but after a couple of requests, he wrote to say that he was unhappy to continue in this role and would I desist. Obviously, I complied with his wishes. But 10 years later, I was covering a Sainsbury AGM at Grosvenor House as a trainee securities analyst and author of two books on the retail sector, I met him again and he was very civil to me.

BRITISH BAKERIES

This bread and cake manufacturer/distributor was, in the 1960s, part of the Rank, Hovis, McDougal (RHM) Group. It launched the Mr Kipling cake brand, which is now part of Premier Foods. British Bakeries Ltd Head Office was in Lime Street in the City of London, next door to Lloyds, the insurance market. This was my first job in the city, and I was so excited that I went straight into Austin Reed in nearby Fenchurch Street; here I bought a bowler hat and a black umbrella (de rigueur in 1960s London). These accoutrements went well with my pin-stripe suit, I thought. But when I stepped out of the store, I realised that I was a clone – every other male in sight was wearing identical garb.

As usual, I had responded to a press advertisement for a retail researcher. The following is an approximate version of the interview, which was conducted by an interviewer and an observer, with particular emphasis on its tone:

Q. First question, Mr Cox: how did you get into Sainsbury?

A. Got the bus to Stamford Street and walked in the door.

Q. Naah! What I mean is – Sainsbury is a very successful and prestigious firm, they don't recruit blindly.

A. How do you mean?

Q. What was it about you, at your age, that made you an attractive hire?

A. I have a first-class degree and experience with Littlewoods as a trainee manager. Also, at NCR, I assessed sites for prospective retail buyers of cash registers.

Q. Yes, but most of these were small firms buying Class 100s, not the new electronic tills.

A. To some extent.

Q. You're not providing us with a particularly helpful picture as to how you could add value to our operation.

A. I'm here to help.

Q. Good. Here's a possible scenario – you are trying to get information from one of our London bakery managers and he challenges you; for example, he suggests that you have not got the experience to do your job, while he has had 30 years at British Bakeries. What is your reaction?

A. I would ask him to give an example of a typical problem he might have in deciding to site a shop, explaining that I have practical experience of this kind of problem – and have even written a book.

Q. But let us say that he wants to know how the shop should be merchandised?

A. No problem. I got a lot of experience on that in Littlewoods, which, of course, has big food halls. The bread and cake sections are carefully located, and performance is monitored through sales conversion factors.

Interviewer: OK. We'll take a chance and offer you the job.

This was my first experience of a "stress" interview. The reason for this palaver, I gathered, was that some bakery managers were "very tough". Could I be a "tactful tiger" with them? Apparently, they thought so. As a relatively young graduate, I found this attitude among field managers in the retail sector to be common. During this period, they were inevitably male, middle-aged, highly experienced in their jobs, but without academic qualifications. Additionally, they might also be suspicious of younger, qualified people who were bright and quick learners or even feel threatened in terms of their jobs. As one employee in another retailer told me: "So-and-so may claim to have 20 years' experience, but it's only one year repeated!" At this time, there was also much hostility to "theory". Fortunately, in the 21st century, things have changed radically, and managers are largely far better trained and educated. As I say to business studies students, in my subsequent second career, "A synthesis of practical experience and a clear understanding of the theory underpinning it is essential for success in any serious job." Incidentally, the upshot of my successful interview was a substantial pay increase and an agreement with the company to adjust my job specification to my experience. A good start, but who knows what the future holds? Incidentally, a basic method of stressing job candidates is simply to reverse the chair they are invited to sit on. The interviewee's immediate response, of course, is to look directly at the panel head, put the chair straight and sit.

My first boss at British Bakeries was Peter Daniels, one of the three best I experienced in the retail industry. It wasn't just that, like the other favourites I had, I was allowed to drive their cars. It is a far greater experience to drive a 3-litre vehicle, rather the one allocated at my level, with half the capacity. As an ex-Marks-&-Spencer manager, Peter was fond of waking up dozing participants at meetings in the company's training centre during the "graveyard shift" after lunch by a reference to his former employer's leadership in bra sales. My job included measuring bakery shop productivity, which covered staffing levels, and the merchandising of very short shelf-life products like cream cakes. Another interesting task was compiling monthly sales data for the Census of Distribution, published by the then

Board of Trade. This annual survey was the only source of information on retail trends in those days. Today, a proliferation of non-government organisations provide constant monitoring of this very changed sector.

Unfortunately, a departmental restructuring replaced Peter with a new boss. His management style and perceived grip on the job irked me, and I was sacked. He was subsequently given the same treatment, but I had to find a new job, especially as our first child, James, had been born.

JOHN MENZIES

Looking back on the handwritten letter I had sent to this company "on spec", in these days of emails, I feel somewhat ashamed. The letter was based on research, which suggested that the company, which had just taken over a similar English business, could use some of the skills that were laid out in my recently published book. I was invited to Edinburgh and was interviewed separately by half a dozen directors, both at Group and subsidiary level, including John Menzies, the chairman. The company had recognised, with dismay, in its publication *The Menzies Group* (1965), the increasing fall in bookshop numbers, and being a bookseller and stationer itself, that this might form part of a growth strategy.

My position was clearly a new one for the company, so I produced a basic job description and styled myself as retail development manager. I then proceeded on a task that I found both fascinating and fulfilling; a dream job, self-designed, where you could see a progression of effort from start to a finish. In essence, it meant identifying towns in Britain where JM stores could effectively operate, followed by site and location assessment and approval, store design and fitting and, finally, merchandising and handing over to field management. I was given an office with a secretary, a clerk and an ex-store manager for merchandising. Outsourcers provided property and shop-fitting advice and support. At about the same time, Menzies had engaged the management consultants Urwick Orr to give advice on strategic planning. The firm fielded one or two young men of my age, who, with my colleagues from finance and marketing, had fruitful dialogues; these often took place in Rose Street, where the company head office was situated – this "street of a hundred pubs" actually only had 18 at the time. Funnily enough, the company name could be pronounced in three different ways in Scotland; paralleling that, it also sported at least three logotypes when I joined.

One of my colleagues, who I considered an important mentor, was a senior accountant and director of one of the London subsidiaries. His advice to me was "In the country of the blind, the one-eyed man is king" and revealed that the company made more money from subletting the offices and flats above its shops than from retailing. So, in effect, John Menzies was more a property business than a retailer. My response to this allegation was that my job was to reverse this situation. But would the consortium of Old Etonians and Scottish Academicals that ran the show go with this? Or did they even care? The late Angus Sharp, who played a blinder as a member of the Blackheath scrum, was the sort of pragmatic, no-nonsense man any business needs. Bless him.

We did succeed in opening some profitable stores in England to compete against the much larger and diversified WHSmith. But there were disasters. Mackie's, a large cake shop and cafeteria in the middle of Princes Street, was up for sale, one of my commercial estate agents informed me. The Board of Directors agreed that opening the chain's potential flagship store in the Scottish capital would be a master stroke. Unfortunately, this ignored that the company ran two smaller stores at either end of the admittedly lengthy and very busy street. The problem, difficult to quantify in a forecast, was cannibalisation. The efforts of various managers to make it pay failed.

For me, working for John Menzies was a wonderful experience. There were many cameo incidents that I shall remember with pleasure, apart from the companionship of many of my colleagues. I refer elsewhere to the trip to Paris, organised by Laing the property and construction group. With a view to assessing the location, I attended the opening of the Paisley shopping mall, opened by James Bond. Sean Connery told a story about his hospitalisation locally following his demob after World War Two. Army patients had to wear special blue suits, white shirts and red ties and so were easily recognisable in the street. With an Edinburgh accent in Glasgow, he was regularly threatened by local bruisers – another reflection of the long-standing enmity between the two Scottish cities, referred to in a previous chapter. On a visit to London with the Menzies chief book buyer, we attended a book launch at Lady Antonia Fraser's home in Holland Park. A charming host, we enjoyed a gracious welcome to her impressive house – one detail remains with me: an Augustus John miniature, alone on the hallway wall.

Then a new man joined the company. His name was John Allen, from Tesco. He was a pleasant guy, who was obviously very experienced in the retail industry. Suddenly, I discovered he was my replacement! Somewhat bemused, I asked my boss Douglas McDonald what was going on. He told me that I had completed my remit, as far as the company and he, as managing director, was concerned. So, that was it. Simon, our second child, had just been born in Lady Margaret's Hospital. What to do? I had been applying for jobs down south for some time, partly due to the misery of my wife Liz since we moved to Scotland. I was not the first senior person to be sacked at this period; a few months earlier, I had accompanied the company surveyor to an empty shop next to M&S in central Croydon. After what seemed to be a thorough examination of the building fabric, it was pronounced as a suitable addition to the JM estate and duly passed on for conveyancing by the company's solicitors. A few days later, the store frontage collapsed into North End; shortly after this, I noticed a job advertisement in *The Times* for the surveyor's position. I told him immediately, but he laughingly denied it. Then he disappeared.

I had some notice and took up Dougie's palliative offer of a farewell lunch with all my colleagues in a good local restaurant. I also began writing my second book based, again, on what I had learned at John Menzies. Thank you, old John Menzies! I use the term "old" because the name now represents a new business in an entirely different industry. It is now an international airline services group and, at the time of writing, like most other worldwide operators in aviation, suffering from the effects of Covid-19. Although the retail part of the Group was sold to W.H. Smith, the wholesale arm continues to operate under the Menzies name. The eponymous airline logistics business is separately owned.

As mentioned previously was hampered by the onset of a lengthy national postal strike. I developed the wheeze of using the internal communication channels of retailers to circulate my CV. A new job had to be in London. Fortunately, most large retailers were based there and, personally, I preferred the South East for its climate and its proximity to London as a cultural centre and international travel hub. For Liz, it was about nearness to old friends and relations, superb shopping and access to beautiful, relatively flat countryside. Eventually, I was offered a consultancy post at a retail firm in Croydon.

ALLIED SHOE REPAIRS

A Division of Allied Leather Industries, based in, could we say, the leather belt in the West Midlands, my new office was in Green Dragon House, South End, Croydon. The post was temporary, for six months, and my remit was to examine merchandising of shoe requisites such as polish, brushes, laces and so forth, as support for the main business of repairs. Again, the emphasis was on productivity improvement, possibly through the introduction of self-service, which was quickly spreading into non-food outlets. My research in many units around the country was incorporated in a comprehensive report to the board. One highlight of my travels was when I visited the Ruislip shop, where the cobbler showed me an assortment of Elton John's boots – he still obviously had a Pinner connection. Like most of the firms I served, Allied has been replaced in the high streets, in this case by Timpson, the tightly-managed shoe repair chain.

After the consultancy stint was over, I had not found a replacement, so, as a supposed retail expert, I had no trouble in joining the College for the Distributive Trades in Leicester Square. As it turned out, this usefully filled in a gap, which was helpful in my career transition, described in the next chapter. My intention was to wow the college students – and lecturers – with tales of battling at the leading edge of the retail revolution, of success and failure. Instead, I was forced to teach book-keeping and statistics. My salary was cut in half, with no expenses, no company car (even the consultancy merited a Vauxhall Saloon). Teaching is a wonderful, fulfilling vocation – that problem solved – but from a material point of view, I have found, it is best teaching post-graduates in private colleges. So I decamped from the College for the Distributive Trades, much to the natural disquiet of Dr Curzon, its principal. He actually harangued the personnel manager of the next company I joined on the phone over my disloyalty. Can you spare a copper or two, guv?

ADA (HALIFAX) LTD

The name comes from a washing machine manufacturer that Philips, the Dutch Group, took over to join its then major domestic appliances division. The function of the company now was to run and, if possible, develop the Group's British retail interests. Like John Menzies, Ada (Halifax) seemed to be searching for help, particularly for its chain of rental TV shops, which totalled 600 when I joined. The company had reacted to a tactical move by competitor Thorn, which had decided to vertically integrate production divisions with distribution channels. This seemed to make sense at the time; controlling instore merchandising and display as well as profit margins by dispensing with "middlemen". Thorn created retailer Rumbelows. "Philips panicked" at this, observed a property director. The real problem for the company was that, as a follower, it picked up hundreds of small shops, many in the wrong places. Most specialised in renting TV sets at a time when consumers were starting to buy their own, as the market expanded and prices fell.

My job, although it was never explicit, was to institute a recovery strategy for the retail division. This would involve a tactical shift into larger store units, which would carry the full range of Philips products – both white (freezers, dishwashers) and brown (TVs, radios) and small appliances. I had access to monthly printouts of each store's financial performance. Combing through the store estate on an extensive visiting programme, I could only identify two suitable units, in Slough and Bolton. Both were large enough but in slightly secondary locations. They were duly fitted out by two competing firms, merchandised and both performed to moderate budgets.

Socially, Ada (Halifax) was great fun. At Head Office in the imposing Chesterfield House, standing on an island site between Bloomsbury Square and Barter Street, I had a superb boss, Bill Benstead-Smith, who, again, was a good mentor. Staff get-togethers were usually on the restaurant boats moored on the North Embankment. For much of the work on the shops' strategy, I was seconded to the Manchester office, run from an old cotton mill in Droylsden. Here, again, there was a friendly and supportive management team. Another venture in what was essentially the retail division of Philips (UK) was Eclipse, a chain of discount electrical goods stores, similar to Comet Radiovision, which is referred to later in this chapter. Its chief executive was Brian Palmer, an enthusiastic and capable Liverpudlian. I was asked to help him and his team in locating possible store sites. This again took me to Northern Ireland, which offered expansion possibilities. This was during the Troubles, and central Belfast was filled with British Army personnel and their vehicles, barricades and other kit. Oddly enough, the only untoward event I saw was an invalid car with three passengers on board.

Brian had a great sense of humour and showed me some documents a would-be Eclipse employee had provided to bolster his chances. This unfortunate gentleman had been turned down because Brian had identified them as a report I had written for "Retail Business", published by the Economist Intelligence Unit. We used to go out together for fine dining in Manchester; at one session, he came across whitebait for the first time and declared that the battered fish was "just like eating fish and chips". He was also a member of the select group of my bosses who happily loaned me their company cars; his was a Ford GT with the Ulster licence FOI 11, which he had altered slightly to form a "cherished" number plate. Driving out of Hull on my way back to Manchester, an artic ahead of me spied the plate and attempted to cut me up. I accelerated past him with the longest horn blast I had ever produced. Then sudden remorse – it set me thinking that for six months, by driving to Manchester on Sunday and returning to Kent on Friday, I was missing family and they me. How was that affecting them? On the other hand, I was driving south in company vans filled with discounted white and brown goods for family and friends. Swings and roundabouts.

One element in the Philips' system, which probably helped it to carry out its long-term reorganisation and refocusing, was its internal audit facility. This acted as a sort of in-house consultancy and was feared, particularly when staff perceived it to be moving in the direction of their departments or subsidiaries. In my case, two gentlemen suddenly appeared in my office and began asking some very basic and disconcerting questions: where is your database? I pointed to a couple of slightly battered filing cabinets; how did I make decisions? I parodied a formula learned in economic analysis. They left.

In any case, bad news was on the horizon. The recovery strategy was too little, too late. My research before joining the company suggested that it was loss-making, and its financial position was worsening. The immediate response was to merge Loyds, as the main shop division was called, with a similar Australian-owned business. I queried the wisdom of merging two weak businesses with Bill, my boss, but he clearly saw it as a logical phase in an exit strategy. Over 40 years later, Philips has focused down from a conglomerate to a health technology specialist. But I am sure that it retains its reputation as a good employer. I was not only given, along with the rest of the sales and marketing team who had lost their jobs, a substantial redundancy payment, but was retained for six months as a consultant on the operation of the company in-house employee shops.

TIME FOR A CHANGE?

My experiences in the retail trades had been sufficient enough to provide a reasonably comfortable life for a family of five. They had also given me useful skills, as well as an exciting career. But the retail industry was beginning to change in a much more radical manner. According to retail property experts, there were already too many shops in the wrong places in Britain. As a result, many were being taken over by larger firms; the latter were more efficient but reduced competition. Consumer tastes were changing and the long economic boom of the 1950s and 1960s was ending in a series of recessions, initially sparked by the oil crisis. Additionally, my job as a retail development adviser was threatened by computer software applied to store siting, design, merchandising and financial appraisal. Reflecting on all this, I began to wonder whether I should be thinking of a change in my career. I was beginning to feel like an actor who has become typecast. I think I had almost coined the title of retail development manager. Looking at the retail scene nearly half a century later, these fears were clearly perceptive. One of the points of this book is to highlight the fact that this sort of perception is shared by modern teenagers. According to a survey by Samsung Europe (*The Times*, 20 August 2020), those who have grown up entirely in the 21st century "expect a life of job-hopping and flexible working", citing social media influencer, app developer and even drone pilot as (note this) technology-influenced jobs.

Naturally, I had never heard of a single one of these at the time. My problem was to assess what transferable skills I possessed for a revived career in the last quarter of the 20th century. Carrying out a personal strength-weakness-opportunity-threat (SWOT) analysis, I decided that either the Stock Market or Media Advertising were possible industries to canvass. I now describe real interviews that I encountered in both sectors.

My first interview was with the Advertising Association, a trade body that represents agencies in the industry. This was held in one of the large terraced houses on the Embankment. As I walked into the interviewing room, I was faced with six or seven males, forming a panel. I had never encountered such a group and nearly burst out laughing, wondering what the point was. I was, in fact, completely put off (perhaps this was the intention). I blurted out: "Good morning, gentlemen, thank you for inviting me – I must say that I'm surprised..." The actual interview lasted about 20 minutes. There were no introductions and no explanation. At roughly the same time, I contacted a large West End agency and told them that Ada (Halifax) needed media help and new ideas. Naively, I expected someone in the agency to contact me for a possible interview, until I discovered that it had taken over the account. Best of luck, I thought.

On to the Stock Market option: A well-known Broad Street broker, which I had written to, graced me with an interview for a retail securities analyst post. On a Friday afternoon, I was ushered in for a chat by the sales partner, who indicated that I should take his seat at the desk. He promptly sat on the other side and put his feet up on it. Most relaxing, I thought. The interview went splendidly, the questions being largely irrelevant or even humorous. I soon realised that the man was drunk. Quite soon, the research partner appeared and quickly took over the farce. The questions immediately became really difficult to answer comprehensively but quite fair for a position of this kind. The younger man disappeared, and the sales partner told me that I had got the job. I hadn't, of course. This occurred in 1976, ten years before "Big Bang", which turned the Market from an old boys' club to the professional organisation it is today. I did write to the Stock Exchange Council to complain; I received a courteous reply, which merely said that the Council could not rule on individual member firm's policies. My next interview for a post of retail securities analyst was successful.

SCOTT GOFF HANCOCK

This stockbroker was also trading in Broad Street, but at the Salisbury Court end. Known as "Gotscoff" by some of my more irreverent, non-city mates, I was recruited as a trainee analyst under John Richards, one of the best retail sector analysts in the city at that time. It was the right period to be joining the Market, at the start of a long boom for share values. A good deal of travel was required, as with my previous jobs. One day we could be chatting in Hull with Michael Hollingberry, the founder of the ill-fated Comet electrical discount chain, the next with Lord Wolfson of Great Universal Stores in Tottenham Court Road. Listening to their views on the retail market and their assessment of their firm's near future in it was exciting and a privilege. Lunches for fund management clients often included guests like Sam Brittan, *Financial Times* correspondent and brother of the late Tory minister. Each in-house lunch started with a large G&T, followed by an excellent meal accompanied first by a good Chablis then by a velvety claret, ending up with a tawny and/or a freezing kummel. Sadly, as I was on probation in the post, it only lasted a year. My problem was that I was not very good at watching people make money, rather than just making it. I did, however, learn many things, such as the difference between market fundamentals and sentiment. I really did enjoy my time there and just before I left, I was able to attend the annual analysts' dinner at the Dorchester. One sad note while writing this: the death of the Rev Gerald Reddington, who was our senior partner before becoming an Anglican priest and a tireless social benefactor in London, as reported in *The Telegraph* (7 August 2020). The firm was subject to several mergers before "Big Bang", notably with Merryll Lynch and, finally, Bank of America.

The simplistic explanation of the current plight of the retail industry is the old complaint of "too many shops in the wrong places". Certainly, the number of shop units has fallen drastically in the last half-century. Shopping centres have also shrunk. In the London area, for example, both Catford and Watford have been decimated by the draws of more powerful retail regional groups, as discussed earlier in this chapter and in the *Financial Times* ("Town proves a shop window on high street woes" 1 September 2020). Here, Allen Leighton, a successful retailer, is quoted in the article: "Every 20 years or so we go through a cycle where there are lots of store openings and then there is a downturn." This has been accentuated by online retail and this time is accelerating as a result of Covid. The growth phase has led to overexpansion of many retailers such as Clinton Cards, John Lewis and even Tesco; the latter had built too many over-large units, which have had to be partially sublet to other retailers. The cost pressures of rents, business rates and state-backed wage increases have caused problems, along with new competition from the likes of hard discounters. Some companies are also loaded with large debt and may even be classed as in a "zombie" status, where they are only paying interest on their loans without reducing the loan itself. But there are retailers who are better managed and more attuned to current – and future – consumer tastes such as Next, Greggs, Waterstones and B&M. The future must involve some of their mindset but will inevitably mean further reduction in retail estates, with ever increasing competition from, for example, Amazon. This will intensify the conversion of shopping into other uses. However, many shops will survive, particularly in low-profit areas like food. Click and collect has helped delivery costs, but Amazon has shown the way by re-opening stateside Toys'R'Us stores for food; allied with its new check-out free technology, where sales are directly debited to customer accounts, its "fresh" policy looks good. (This according to both The Times and the Financial Times).

Although not a retailer, Scott Goff is clearly linked, in my case, to the sector. This chapter also tries to explain how I tried to engineer my career transition to teaching, which is fully discussed next.

Chapter 9

TEACHING

Conventionally, people entering the teaching profession have undertaken various courses designed to implant the skills, knowledge and attitudes required for success in it. I have had no such experience but have relied on my background in management, copious writing, preparing and writing talks delivered at conferences, sometimes at my own Retail Conference events. Coupled with that, I have appeared on both television and radio. My consultancy work is treated in a later chapter.

This chapter describes my experiences in over 40 different universities and colleges, where I taught at Higher Education levels, largely on a freelance level. The places of work are not discussed in chronological order like the retail businesses.

Holborn College:

At its foundation, this institution was based in the eponymous district of the capital. At this point, I taught A Level Economics for only a couple of terms, and it was an initial attempt to tackle the Further Education market, some 20 years after graduation. A few months afterwards, I met one of the students from the class. "How did it go?" I enquired. "We all failed, you weren't very good", came the uncompromising response. This really shook me up and punctured my complacency. The fact that I had never taken a course in teaching methods was hardly an excuse. Notwithstanding this, I was able to follow the college through two more reincarnations. It had moved to an old school in Baron's Court, near Queen's Tennis Club. To drive from the Kent-Surrey border to arrive for a class at 9am was difficult, even allowing two hours – the fight was to get over one of the bridges. I was frequently late, and one Russian student (a very bright guy) used to storm round the college, shouting "Where is he!" More time was spent calming him and the principal. In spite of this, I rejoined the college in its third location on the other side of London, at Charlton. This was far easier for me to drive to. The site had formerly been occupied by Woolwich College, which had taken over an old school site. As if to reflect these changes, the staffing was handled by a completely different set of people. As usual, I was teaching management. My only strong memory was a very attractive female Japanese student.

The College of Management and Marketing Studies (CMMS):

"A Chinaman's College in a Crypt!" spluttered the tousled young man in a public school accent. As I entered the Streatham Church, near the edge of Tooting Bec Common, the bystander's comment seemed like a headline from *Private Eye*. CMMS had been first established in the mid-1970s by Mike Wooi, a clever and affable man, part of a small group of academic refugees from the troubled London South East College. Its immediate success triggered a move to premises above the post office at Tooting Bec. Focusing on teaching the Certificate and Diploma stages of the Association of Business Executives, a successful outcome forms the basis from which an application for a Master's degree could be made. This offering attracted many overseas students (and similar syllabuses publicised by the many other private colleges opening in London at the time) and they came in waves, often reflecting rapid rises in real incomes in each country – Turks, Thais, Nigerians, Chinese, Indians, Russians and East Europeans. Continued success prompted a further move – yes – to old school premises on the edge of Wandsworth Common. CMMS became an associate of the University of Miami and its London campus. Sadly, CMMS went into liquidation in 1986.

The London School of Foreign Trade (LSFT):

As a major centre for world trade, it was fitting that London would host a specialist college that would provide qualifications for foreign students who sought a career in shipping and export. The student body was largely drawn, as would be expected, from Greece, Norway, Finland, Iceland and similar nations with strong mercantile marine interests. Oddly, the numbers of UK citizens were low, certainly in the years I taught there. I was offered a lectureship, partly because I had the same degree as the principal. LSFT was located within the well-known adult-education-oriented Morley

College, situated in Westminster Bridge Road. This college boasts a John Bratby mural (a friend has a portrait of Spike Milligan by this sadly neglected painter). Dressed in a blazer and flannels, one day I was assaulted by a North African gentleman, shouting insults against "the English". When he was quietly led away, it was explained that he "got excited" occasionally. I enjoyed my 10 years or so at this civilised institution, and the students were a joy to teach. Many insisted on taking photographs of me while teaching, and I still treasure the portfolio. The student parties were a frequent feature in the college and in the local, which had had Charlie Chaplin as a patron. When my daughter left school, I managed to install her in the office to carry out her two-week work experience – she loved it there. Unfortunately, in spite of changes of management, LSFT consistently failed to cover its costs and so the Trustees reluctantly closed it. One of the saddest sights was in the window of the Annex, where a picture of an argosy was captioned "The Last Voyage". Vale

Schiller International University:

Quite near to LSFT, and at the south end of Waterloo Bridge, facing the Imax Cinema, the university was housed in the former Women's and Children's Hospital.
It was founded by a German academic, who died only a few years ago. Like all the educational organisations I worked for, Schiller attracted a very multinational student body. But here, I hardly remember a single British student. This must have been due to the fact that its curricula and teaching methods were US-based. Students could not earn a "First", only an "A" – grades were calculated

numerically. Some of the British lecturers, like myself, found it difficult, even irksome, to adjust to American booklists and administration. Richard Taylor, the affable director, sent us red memos when we were seen as ignoring the system, and I had a bundle of them. On the other hand, the atmosphere was academic – Richard was an authority on Thomas Hardy, one of my favourite authors, for instance. But conversely, the culture was friendly, with plenty of social intercourse. Both BBAs and MBAs were taught, but one Jordanian student questioned me about the validity of this ranking, suggesting that he found the Master's degree easier than the Bachelor's!

One day, I was approached in the university by two Turkish gentlemen who expressed concern about the likelihood of one of my students (also Turkish) passing his finals. They invited me to the Conroy Hotel at Chelsea Harbour for breakfast one morning. Suspicious, I ordered a pair of kippers while they offered my wife and me a holiday at a luxury hotel in a Turkish sea resort. I was non-committal but said I would see what I could do. As it transpired, the student's final examination results were satisfactory. We did not take up the offer of a holiday. (I'm glad to note that this sort of situation was very rare in my 40 years of teaching.) Students often wanted to find out more about how British people lived, and I often entertained them – particularly Africans – when I was in London. On one occasion, when I was taking my Master's, I invited the entire class of 16 to lunch in my garden in Westerham on a beautiful summer day; my wife Liz provided lunch and I sorted out the Soave. Students often betrayed their feelings. A girl from Moscow, wearing a "Teddy Bear" knapsack, popular at the time, cried to me about "her Russia" and

Yeltsin. A Brazilian confessed to me that she wished her country had been conquered by the Spanish as "we have such a silly language!" One of the most important members of the university's staff was David, in charge of reception; he was a pleasant, well-educated Orthodox Jew. One day, he told me he was planning a trip with his family to Northern Italy: "You know Como, don't you?" "Yes," I replied and mentioned a five-star hotel at Bellagio, where the food was excellent. "Oh, we'll be taking our own food," he responded with a smile.

Attached to the university, which was based in Miami and had branches all over Europe (e.g. in Paris, Berlin, Madrid and Switzerland), was London City College. This was in the same building as Schiller and was designed as an entrée. I taught mostly export management here. The university moved some years ago and was accommodated in the nearby University of the South Bank (which itself was spawned from a bakery college). The important road junction outside the old Schiller site was known as the Bull Ring, which still has pedestrian subways, and the Imax Cinema stands on previously open area. For a time, this was partially occupied by a "cardboard city", peopled by the homeless. The close proximity of Waterloo Station also generated a huge volume of pedestrians, with the inevitable buskers and hucksters. One tall and ravaged-looking old lady sang *Horsey, horsey* in a not untuneful but harrowing tone that really evoked pity. The appliance box encampment was cleared for redevelopment, and many of the homeless moved into the crypt of St John's Church nearby. As I parked my car outside the church, I got to know a few of these men (no women). One was an ex-nurse, he told me, whose marriage had failed. Like a surprising number of people who are homeless but have acceptable shelter, he confessed that his was the ideal life. From time to time, and particularly at Christmas, I gave cash and cans of beer to the little community, which included all age groups. Their presence attracted "fake beggars", all young, to sit against the church railings – unappreciated, in various ways, by the "sitting tenants". Incidentally, the car parking was sometimes shared by a Saab owned by a fellow lecturer; normally this marque is bought by motorists who try to assume a low profile, but in this case, it carried a "cherished" licence plate – a sort of motoring oxymoron. Just a puzzle. Ian can sue me.

More seriously, the new Director, Doctor Liz Nunn was instrumental in awarding me my honorary doctorate from the University.

London Metropolitan University:

While searching for material to supplement this memoir, I happened upon a pay-slip dated 1966, issued by The City of London College, located in Moorgate, EC2. Initially, as a part-time lecturer, I taught economics to Institute of Transport evening students. My boss was Mr Stebbings, a friendly and helpful man, who generally reflected the atmosphere in the college at that time. It was the primary educational institution in the City of London, serving the Square Mile, even then vying with New York to be the leading global financial hub. Since then, the college has grown and altered substantially, spawning sub-campuses in the city. This has been reflected in three name changes: first, it became City Polytechnic, then London Guildhall University and, finally, after a merger with North London University – London Metropolitan University.

My ultimate boss there for many years was Owen Palmer, who I would class as one of the three mentors I had over my careers. He was head of the Marketing Faculty, and I taught various levels of the Chartered Institute of Marketing syllabus, leading to the MCIM professional qualification. Owen was my protector when I ran into an unfortunate teaching situation with a very large class in a lecture theatre at the Tower Bridge Campus. Two very bright but disputatious students started to wreck the meeting. In my interest in their ideas, I stupidly ignored the rest of the class, who were clearly unamused. One of the disruptors was the daughter of a very senior administrator in the university. I was reported for losing control of the class and summarily removed from teaching it. Owen took over the class and smoothed over the upset. I later resumed teaching the class – the two protagonist had left it. I obviously blamed myself for this lapse but felt that the design of the typical lecture hall can affect perception and communication. The angle of rake is crucial as well as its depth – a presenter can look like a "dot in a pit". Additionally, a three-hour lecture that is not broken out into tutorials can accentuate a lack of the vital feedback. All this occurred nearly 30 years ago and, hopefully, is a thing of the past. Andy Inglis, another helpful guy, fed back to me the CIM exam results each year afterwards, and they were always majority passes, I'm pleased to say.

The Open University:

I joined the part-time teaching fraternity at the OU in 1986. The institution was founded in the late 1960s and was the first international direct-learning-focused university in the world. It not only catered for people who have little or no academic qualifications but was a haven for those that love teaching – or the sound of their own voices – without worrying too much about the monetary benefits. It was a joy to work for an organisation that was well organised, friendly and provided excellent course material. The university is proud of the fact that the latter is often adopted for use by others; I certainly took advantage of it, particularly for teaching on MBA courses. I initially began teaching basic marketing in venues stretching from Guilford to Maidstone to Brighton and to the London HQ in Finchley Road. My boss operated from Regional HQ in East Grinstead. One of the many bright students I encountered at this stage was the British CEO of a US medical electronics company. His final submission to pass the module was one of the best pieces of coursework I had ever marked – beautifully structured, well researched and reasoned. I awarded it 76 per cent. My boss, who second-marked it, asked, "Why not give it 96 per cent if it was so good?" (Code for: comments must be mirrored by mark). The British convention was that if it's over 70, that's a First or Distinction. His point was that it was a waste not to use the full range to reflect comparative performance up to super-excellent. That also helps "ranking". This revelation altered my attitude to marking for ever.

Apart from the work I was doing in the south-eastern region of the university, I was asked in 1992 to teach on the new OU Master of Business Administration (MBA), as I had already earned a Master's degree in management. This took me all over the country, mostly at weekends, each month. Because my original family lived in the

Manchester area, I visited UMIST to lecture on the MBA. This is now part of the University of Manchester. The building that we used was part-conference centre; facilities are good, except that many of the guest rooms only have en suite showers. The guest comments book contained a question from a female student: "Do I have to stand on my hands to properly bathe myself?" Another external facility explained to us in a briefing was: "When you go out of an evening, you will find two areas, the pink zone and the red zone: the first is obviously the Gay Area and the other is 'the ladies of the night area.'". Out of curiosity, many of us went round to the first area, seeing several pubs with amorous males sitting close together. In nearby Canal Street, the first letters of each word had been expunged from the street sign. As to the other zone, one of my tutor colleagues reported jogging there at 6.30am, only to be accosted by a young lady who enquired whether he would "like a nice time". At nearby Salford University, on another occasion, I was trying to run an OU course during a riot at Strangeways Prison; we could see and hear activity on the roof during the whole weekend. For a quieter experience, I would recommend a visit to the magnificent machine hall in the university.

To illustrate what a fairly typical weekend course would be like, the following is an actual example: An introduction and briefing session starts the group contact on Friday afternoon. Groups are 12 strong, to help general communication and break-outs. One of the students was a physician from a Manchester hospital, and by Saturday lunch-time, a couple of other members complained that he had flatly refused to take part in his sub-group's analysis of a case study. I am a great believer in self-help in these situations and asked them to sort it out; one was the truck buyer for a large chemical group. The following morning, they came to me and told me that the problem had been solved. Apparently, they had taken the doctor into the bar and got him so drunk that he had agreed to participate. On Sunday afternoon, after informed presentations from all three groups, I debriefed the class, and we said our farewells. At the very end, the reformed character came up to me and said: "I have learned one thing on this course." "Please tell me," I responded. "I now believe that management is just acting!" I had to admit, he had a point.

I left the OU 20 years after joining, with some regret. As I have indicated, it was a wonderful period, and I learned a great deal. My objection is personal and may well be disputed by policy makers. I had taught strategic management for over 10 years at the OU. This module is the most overarching one taught on the MBA and covers wide operational links, organisational and cultural concerns. If possible, when a single case study is to be analysed by student groups, over the weekend, it should touch on as many of these aspects as possible, I believe. In this regard, I was summoned in the middle of the first decade to Head Office, Milton Keynes; here I was briefed on a case study to be introduced on weekend courses. It involved the launch of a new medical product by a pharmaceutical company; this meant a focus on marketing, a strategic support. But, additional to a marketing plan, the launch was to be aided by scenario prediction. This technique, developed by Shell in 1977, involves the development of alternative "futures" in a particular sector. The problem was that case took a very narrow view of the strategic remit and, to me, was a poor simulation for students on the then Module B881. To be brutally frank, it appeared to be obsessed with the ideas of scenarios and marketing. It may well be that this perceived flaw in such cases has been attended to subsequently. Just one extra interesting point about adult education, which does not just affect the OU; a few students do not necessarily attend for the sole purpose of earning a qualification. I was propositioned more than once, in circumstances quite different from the jokey ones I trotted out when being interviewed for a place at 47 Weymouth Street in Chapter 6.

Greenwich School of Management:

GSM was founded in 1973. When the London School of Foreign Trade folded in 1992, I had already made two attempts to join the former. I finally managed it in January of the latter year, and on my first day, I faced a revolution. Arriving in the correct classroom in what had been the former Greenwich Town Hall, I noted that students who had just arrived were now filing out of the college front doors. The Greek Head of School, in an obviously pre-arranged plan, was taking as many students as possible to a new college in Docklands. I was standing behind Gerald and William Hunt, the proprietors, who seemed powerless to halt the absconding. The students were guided through the Greenwich foot tunnel to the Crossharbour area of the Isle of Dogs on the other side of the Thames. The last time I had seen the area was when I took a group of students from LSFT to see the plans for Canary Wharf and its miraculous transition to the second "City of London". The students were bound for the brand-new

London campus of Western International, a Phoenix, Arizona, university, only one of a horde of US educational institutions that saw London as easy meat. This story tells a different tale, but William told me later that it had taken two years for GSM to recover financially.

Morale, however, was quickly on the uptake and the college soon regained a relaxed and happy atmosphere. The Hunts allowed the teaching staff space to operate as they wished, within obvious guidelines. Bureaucracy was scorned, particularly by Dr Gerald Hunt, who had been Chancellor of Aston University (and his first degree was the same as mine). Mention of the Americans in London, above, must refer to the same expansion of British universities in the same direction. In this regard, GSM became a franchisee of the University of Hull. We taught their degrees and provided our own study materials. Hull presided over examination boards in order to monitor the quality of our degree classifications at both Bachelor and Master levels. In order to refine assessment, academics from other British universities, such as St Andrews and Middlesex, were invited. One of the unique selling points of GSM was its two-year "express" first degree courses, taught over six equal semesters, with short breaks in between. At the same time, fees were only two-thirds of the then £9,000 per term required by other universities. As a result, the college gained a reputation for improving social mobility and attracting disadvantaged students, not only from Britain but from all parts of Africa, particularly. On the downside, some students failed to realise that they needed to work much more intensively, due to the time constraints and lower fees.

Over time, GSM had accumulated a strong teaching faculty, with a number of ex-business managers to infuse the essential theory side of academic studies with real stories of how commerce copes with its never-ending problems, and how opportunities can be successfully grasped. Very few lecturers were sacked, not just for lack of teaching skills and empathy towards students or, in one case, losing examination papers on the Tube, but for open racialism – unforgiven in multicultural groups. Hull later ended their links with GSM, partly due to problems in their Business Faculty. In spite of that, a couple of its lecturers continued to work for us. In order to continue a franchise link, Gerald thought, quite correctly, that there was safety in numbers and negotiated and signed contracts both with the new University of Wales (based on the old Pontypridd Polytechnic) and the University of Plymouth. In the former case, there were links to other London institutions; the arrangement was terminated later by GSM. The Plymouth connection, signed in 2006, was an excellent choice for GSM. It enabled me and various colleagues to visit its campus on several occasions, including degree-awarding ceremonies. We got on well with the staff there, and its culture and ambiance were impressive. The university (formerly a polytechnic) was voted "the best new university " on occasion; it was particularly lauded for its marine studies and for entrepreneurship support. Examination Boards were generally more relaxed than with Hull. On one occasion, John Lipcynski, an economist colleague, and I were involved with the evaluation and launch of a new economics degree and received much praise for our contribution. John and I ran many Executive MBA sessions at weekends for business managers. Our special expertise was in corporate strategy. One of the pleasures flowing from this was the many chance meetings in London with students who had developed successful businesses, based on the knowledge and experience gained from their EMBAs.

On the teaching side, at times some of us were putting in 70 hours a week of student contact alone. One lecturer earned nearly £20,000 in a single month and was feted by the managing director over a bottle of Pol Roger.

By the end of the first decade of the century, GSM was performing well. Lord Harris of Peckham had bequeathed a new library and the college was on track to recruit 6,000 students. This success attracted the attention of a private equity group, Sovereign Capital, which had already invested in education providers. The subsequent inflow of funds enabled GSM to expand to three campuses, one in Tabard Street, Borough (near London Bridge), and another in Greenford Road, Greenford, in a former GSK unit, both additional to the main College in Royal Hill, Greenwich. The idea was to provide a Pan-London Group, covering its east, west and centre, thus increasing the college catchment area. Substantial renovation and upgrading of the Greenwich site was undertaken, providing lecture theatres, a hugely extended library, a student hub area and electronic gates. Similar improvements were made at the other two campuses. Academically, new syllabuses were introduced, particularly in Law, Economics and Oil and Gas Studies. A plan was mooted for the adoption of University College status, which would allow GSM to offer its own degrees. By 2017, the GSM turnover was in excess of £37 million, partly due to tuition fee changes, introduced in 2010. The future appeared to look good, particularly the boost that the Blair Government had instituted, which had increased school-leaver participation in Higher Education to over 40 per cent (when I was an undergraduate in the 1950s, that figure was barely 5 per cent).

The first public signs of a problem were revealed in *The Sunday Telegraph* ("Battle to save college network from collapse", 26 August 2018). In November 2017, it was implicated in a BBC investigation into a student loans fraud. At this time, Lloyds Bank waived £21 million in long-term lending to the college to try to prevent its collapse. The end came less than two years later. The *Financial Times* headline on 2 August 2019 was "Students learn bitter lessons from GSM London failure". The student rolls had fallen from 6,000 to 3,500, and the newspaper pointed out that its plight highlights the pressures facing a number of Higher Education institutions. GSM also missed out on registering with the new Office for Students, which would have guaranteed the Government's student loan package – a main source of potential income. Over the next two years, the impact of Covid-19 further impacted on the crucial financial stability of many HE institutions, many of which are heavily indebted. I have dwelt at length on this particular educational institution because I spent 27 years serving it. In a letter published by the *Financial Times*, editorially headed "HE reform should focus on managerial capacity" (6 August 2019), I suggest that the future of many of these institutions will be determined by the quality of its leadership, with the rider that useful experience and advice can even be found in their own lecturing faculties.

Western International University:

WIU was set up in Phoenix, Arizona, in 1978, and in the early 1990s opened a campus in London's redeveloping Docklands. The centre of the main area, known as Canary Wharf, sits the New-York-style César Pelli skyscraper. WIU initially set up shop in the cheaper Crossharbour sector and, as related in the previous section, quickly gathered a large number of students by questionable means from GSM. As freelance lecturers, three or four other colleagues and I followed the students over the Thames and spent two or three years teaching at WIU. This was known by the Hunt brothers at GSM, and there was no overt objection from them. Possibly we were seen as spies within a nearby competitor. Although the campus was modern and pleasant, the student numbers (in spite of the Greenwich influx) remained modest. The syllabuses, teaching style and marking system were, thankfully, not Americanised (as at Schiller). However, we had constant visits from Phoenix-based administrators. The principal, who apparently possessed an English Literature doctorate, liked London for his own reasons and was around a lot, occasionally accompanied by his spouse. We could sense that there were financial difficulties, because the campus moved twice after leasing its original home. The last building the university occupied was slightly damaged when a lorry containing an IRA bomb exploded. The London branch of WIU entered administration twice, within about a year. I attended the first creditors' meeting, but it was a complete waste of time; presumably the wherewithal to continue trading had been found from somewhere, but we were given no feedback. I did not bother to go to the second meeting, because I was lucky – a Thai student completed his dissertation, handed it in and I marked it a pass. The fees were still good – around $1,000. I invoiced Phoenix HQ and received a cheque that was cashable. The university had been part of the US Apollo Education Group, and new owners decided to close WIU due to declining enrolment and revenue in March 2017.

Polytechnics/Universities:

My own HE teaching extended over a period when polytechnics were morphing into universities. Teaching at South Bank Polytechnic for the then Institute of Marketing Diploma coincided with Holly Johnson's BBC-banned single in 1983. At the same time, I was studying for an MA at Thames Polytechnic (to be Greenwich University, 10 years on). This degree in management was awarded by courtesy of the Council for National Academic Awards i.e. before polys could issue their own degrees. The CNAA degree was quite rigorous; a cohort of 38 students at the start was reduced to 16 after interim exams, and only three of us completed on time – me and two Nigerian students. As a reward, I was allowed to teach marketing at Thames for a year. Similar posts were available and filled by me at the new Guildhall and Westminster Universities. I also taught sales promotion at the University of East London.

The Oxford Street area: I taught in four colleges in this part of central London during the late 1970s and early 1980s. One was next to a large store, which sported a huge "closing down" notice in its window for over a year – as a retailer, I thought this could be an attractive sign for a multiple store group. It has been mentioned before, but at this time, private FE education was dominated by the Greek nationality. One college in James Street, opposite Bond Street, was operated by a Greek gentleman; I taught there for a year until he suddenly decamped to Salonika, never to be seen again.

Borough:

This Southwark high street is my favourite in all London – it typifies the old city and is a bit of an education hub. At the peak is the Blue Plaque on John Harvard's old house. Queen's Head Yard contained an accountancy spin-off from CMMS, which I lectured in, near Kaplan, in which I did not. At the corner of Tabard Street was the London Institute of Technology Research, where I worked for a year or two but which is now apparently derelict. Another grandiosely named institute on the other side of the High Street was The College of Advanced Studies, where you could presumably obtain doctorates.

Croydon College:

I failed to obtain a full-time post at Croydon, which would have been easy for me to drive to. They offered and I accepted some evening lecturing. The gentleman who beat me to the main post was subsequently found, at another college, not to have earned the BSc (Econ.) he claimed to have.

"Crammers":

One of these colleges for failed accountancy examinees was just off what is now known as "Silicon

Roundabout". Here I was summarily sacked when one student, in the very small class, complained that I referred too much to my notes. (I decided at this early point in my teaching career to memorise a complete course in management which I could deliver in a day, week, month or semester; it worked like a treat and students often marvelled at the ability to talk hard facts without pause for an hour or more). Oddly enough, at another similar college next to the Old Bailey, I was interviewed and appointed to a teaching post by the very man who had fired me in City Road; he also commissioned me to write a teaching manual on economics!

Other Institutions:

Several other London venues I have taught at include Regent's College, Kensington College, Lansdowne College, Martran College, and un-named institutions at the Angel, Islington, Seven Sisters Road and Clapham Common. I have also taught from time to time at the Chartered Institute of Marketing at its headquarters at Cookham in Berkshire. The following section describes some of my experiences as a senior examiner of the organisation.

As an examiner, I provided examination papers for the Sales and Sales Management Module at the Certificate Level of the course. At one examiners' meeting at Cookham, I was woken by the chief examiner, who was apparently complaining about the latest draft paper I had submitted. The accompanying case study was based on a Birmingham motor distributor and discussed how a branch network in a large city could benefit from adroit selling, backed by appropriate promotional support. To be fair, Birmingham, a motor city, is part of the ethnically diverse West Midlands conurbation; but perhaps mention in the case of names such as Balsall Heath or Edgbaston might put examinees off? Anyway, the chief tartly suggested that because the paper was aimed at international students in a worldwide network, as well as the British, the case study was far too parochial for its purpose. Panicking, I swiftly produced a new case based on a mythical South Korean manufacturer of the new, fashionable "Soldier" 4WD. Fortunately, the revised paper was accepted. I enjoyed marking the exam scripts for this module and was particularly pleased to be able to pass one entry from a New York penitentiary. Unfortunately, the module was subsequently dropped due, I believe, to low take-up.

I joined the then Institute of Marketing in 1980, subsequently becoming a Fellow 20 years later. At the same time, I joined the Marketing Education Group, designed for people teaching the subject. At one of its meetings, the main speaker, Dr Malcolm McDonald, suggested that I sign up for a PhD at his workplace, Cranfield University. This I did and Malcolm offered to be my supervisor, which I readily agreed to. For my first review, I was summoned to Cranfield, which is in Bedfordshire, to face a panel of six or seven professors. I had submitted a section of a possible thesis, largely outlining its rationale. Much of the discussion involved the difficulties of successfully pursuing a doctorate; this was illustrated by anecdotes of how marriages had failed, serious mental problems had developed and that my efforts reflected those of "a talented MSc student". I gathered from all this that similar meetings were part of the compensatory enjoyment that university dons got against their miserly earnings and the sheer drudgery they had to submit to from time to time. When I was reminded that it would probably take seven years for me to graduate, I mentally decided there and then to drop out. Apart from this, attending classes in this pre-Zoom era, or even meetings with my supervisor, required a 160-mile round trip. I concluded that to take a conventional PhD required me to be younger than my then 50+ years, and to be teaching in the university, with easy access to staff, the library and the right environment. There was a sort of compensation for me. Schiller International University decided to award me a Doctor of Humane Literature degree (the equivalent of a D.Litt.) for my five published books. But it wasn't the university that gave me the "Honorary Doctorate", because the degree certificate I was given expressly states that only Bachelor's and Master's degrees are awarded. So the London Campus Faculty kindly carried out the honour at a normal graduation ceremony next door in an annex of King's College. One of my friends looked at the degree description and said: "It's DHL!" Oh dear.

What of the future? In my view, it was a mistake to convert polytechnics into universities, blurring the important distinction between tertiary and Higher Education. With half of school leavers entering HE studies, many graduates are not employed in graduate jobs. A fair proportion of these would have benefitted from a technical education, which could have created much-needed electricians and engineers. In turn, they would probably have been happier, and productivity in this country, which lags that in similar European and other states, might have been improved. To put it brutally, many degrees are a waste of time and money. Another concomitant problem is the overexpansion of the university sector, not only in operational unit sizes, but also in numbers – around 150 in Britain today. Their development has created substantial indebtedness; the fate of GSM in Greenwich could be a bellwether, particularly taking the effects of Covid-19 into account. Students in some institutions have complained of poor teaching. Gone almost entirely is the idea that the possession of a university degree was a sign of a certain level of intellectual ability and that learning was a goal in itself. Another contentious, slightly connected thought is that academics tend to be good administrators but poor managers. The Government's latest idea, announced at the end of September 2019, is to boost STEM, or technical subjects, in the educational sphere. For people without an A Level or equivalent qualification, a grant-aided Open-University-style is mooted, with more support for those who want to go straight to undergraduate level. Hopefully, the curious idea of MBA apprenticeships will be dropped; but certainly not the latter itself. In reality, businesses say that they want to develop short, flexible apprenticeship courses mixing work experience and skills ("boot-camps"), with college delivery, by better utilising the levies they pay for this, according to both The Times and Financial Times.

Chapter 10

CONSULTANCY

Before describing the "real" consulting I carried out, I should dwell a little on the various jobs I did after I moved to London. For the room in our Central London flat, I was paying £4 a week, but salaries were low, too. At NCR, I started at £900 a year (Littlewoods in Edinburgh paid £600). One or two of my flatmates, giving away their salary levels, declared that anyone earning less than £2,000 was a failure; it took me another three or four years to hit this level. As a result, I began what is known as "moonlighting" to bolster my main earnings. There was some teaching available, but as I had managed to buy my first car, a second-hand Morris Minor, I decided to try selling. There were three London evening newspapers at the time, and the *Standard* was good on jobs. My first was with the Encyclopedia Britannica, which had an office in Vauxhall Bridge Road; here I was given a swift training course in selling the children's version. We were advised to introduce ourselves as local authority education officers and enquire whether there were children of school age in the family. Of course, such an approach today would be laughable; we were never challenged, asked for any identification, and entry was almost always gained. We were also advised to land on better-off areas, particularly in North London – Primrose Hill was a likely target. After a spiel about the multi-volume publication (which cost hundreds of pounds), we would sit down beside the prospect and eventually present them with an order form, followed by the handing over of a pen, which was inevitably taken. The trap was set. I was immediately suspicious of this approach because in 1963, there was no time for client reflection and no obligatory trial period. There was virtually no consumer protection at this time, and as a result, I made little attempt to persuade families to buy. In fact, I was so appalled by what I was supposed to be doing that I wrote a stern letter to *New Society*, pointing out the iniquities of this sales process. The letter was given high prominence in its correspondence column and, hopefully, helped bring in the avalanche of consumer protection legislation of the late 1960s and the 1970s.

After my resignation from the "Britannica", I saw an advertisement for car owners who would take students out of an evening to sell canned dog food. Before I went to interview, I checked in several supermarkets whether they stocked much pet food, and the answer suggested not. Arriving at an office in Soho, I found a crowd of students looking at a large map of North London (again, supposedly more fertile ground for rich consumers). A man with a pointer indicated the areas that could be visited – Palmer's Green, for example. I wondered whether this guidance had been based on any local research, but before I could potentially blow the sales campaign out of the water, the man with the pointer asked me (without any identification offered or requested) to gather some students and several cases of dog food, load my car and proceed northward. I meekly obeyed without querying, for example, what the insurance arrangements were for the car occupants, and off we went into the winter's night. Over the next week or two, my team and I sold several cases of dog food at one shilling and ninepence for each tin. We knocked on doors at random, asking each household whether they kept a dog or dogs. Unfortunately, I wrote off my car in Manchester on a visit to my parents, thus ending another career. Some 20 years later, after I had left the security of a permanent job to go freelance, I decided to try mini-cabbing, largely in the evenings, as I had begun teaching business studies in private colleges.

Some local work with Beeline in Sevenoaks, which provided vehicles, allowed me to drive the only London "Black Cab" the company had down to Tunbridge Wells and so on. This was tame stuff, and a friend suggested that I join him with SLG, a big firm operating from Sydenham. Here you had to supply your own vehicle; at that time, I had a two-door Toyota Corolla estate – its former feature was bad for min-cabbing, but the latter was an advantage. Anyway, they fitted the car with a two-way radio and arranged insurance, both at a cost to me. Remuneration was based on my retaining a percentage of fares collected. Much of my work was in the evening because of teaching during the day. It took me all over the country, as SLG had many accounts, often with large clients. Frequent trips from the ICL factory in Sydenham, taking computer parts, for example to GCHQ in Cheltenham. This was interspersed with taking late-night computer workers from city banks to their homes in Essex. Driving worse-for-wear journalists from Fleet Street back to Kent was an ongoing feature. On one occasion, I was beaten up by a drunk at a Forest Hill pub, whose mate rushed out to pay me off before my assailant put me in hospital.

Like Sean Connery, I also delivered milk in Edinburgh, but exasperated readers will be saying, rightly, that this is not consultancy – so here goes, real business consultancy: Retail Conferences was an unincorporated business designed to highlight and explain new trends in distribution. For example, in 1979, there was growing interest in EFTPOS (electronic funds transfer at point-of-sale), as a means not only of controlling cash but also stock. First, I researched potential markets for client sources; retailing itself had many divisions from multiples to independents, then sectors like hospitality, banking, fuel distribution, entertainment and many other services. Second, I chose top-class London venues with good conference and banqueting facilities, such as the Park Lane Hilton, Kensington Garden and the Café Royal. Third, as a long-term reader of the *Financial Times*, I took small advertising spaces in it. Fourth, speakers were friends of friends (IBM produced some), retail marketing experts and city analysts. I even tried to entice some well-known politicians. At this time, the Social Democratic Party was being formed, and this appealed to me, as Labour was becoming less and less attractive. As a result, I invited Shirley Williams to speak, but she declined graciously. Background notes were provided by individual speakers; I compered the sessions, assisted by friends' wives or, occasionally, by my students. Some speakers provided videos, one of which showed an early application of the system in a gas station in Fresno; all additionally supported their talks with hard copy.

After a few months, we had over a hundred clients, which were listed on a publicity brochure, ranging from banks to oil companies.

Roy Hattersley, the Labour minister, was invited to speak at one session. When he failed to appear, without any notice, his slot was ably filled by a young IBM manager who was also a main speaker. Years later, Mr Hattersley played the same trick on the BBC TV programme HIGNFY. In tune with its humour, his panel chair was filled with a large slab of lard. Another topic that was of growing importance in the distributive sector was fast food, or *restauration rapide*, as the French called it. After all, the British "burger industry" was a mere 15 years old, with the opening of the first McDonald's outlet in Woolwich. The main speaker in this conference, held in the Hilton, was the marketing manager of KFC. He provided an interesting and insightful overview of his franchise; this even included dealing with "unofficial" sales promotion material, which often appeared in individual units. A sectoral view was ably provided by Nick Bubb, today a highly rated independent city analyst. This conference was unique in two respects: first, the attendees only just out-numbered the speaker line-up, and second, it was the last event run by this business. The reasons for both were created by the onset of the 1980–82 business downturn. This, along with my experience as a trainee analyst in the city, intensified my interest in business cycles. It led to my attempts to forecast the next serious economic recession 10 years later.

After years of learning by doing and listening to field managers and trainers, you gain a feel for public speaking.

FROM PRACTICE TO THEORY

As someone who had learned much about how the retail industry works, I was often asked to present to large audiences (this is no place for advice, which can be found in thousands of ways – practice is, of course, vital). On one occasion, representing a research agency, I was greeted by one of its directors, who introduced me to the audience. His name was Mr Shute, and at our first meeting, he thrust his hand out at arm's length, aiming at my midriff, and shouted out his name. Furthermore, at the end of my talk, he noted that I had mis-spelt the word "hierarchy" on my flip chart. Sometimes speakers are not re-invited. Again at the Beaumont Conference Centre at Windsor, I had to address a huge gathering of ICL Computer salespeople. Striding toward the podium, I was suddenly halted by an end-seat delegate who told me that the John Lewis logo had been printed upside down in my latest book. I quickly owned up and recommenced my tramp to the platform. I began my talk by thanking the interrupter and apologising to any readers present who had spotted the error. At a much more recent Co-op venue in the Midlands, I was glad to see Paul, the co-author of my latest book published. Here, without prior warning, I was involved in a televised interview on my views on Marks & Spencer and its problems. Sometime later, I recorded a talk on Essex Radio on general trends in mall shopping. While working with Wellcome, before its merger with Glaxo and on behalf of the OU, I was televised by the BBC. I was supervising an in-company course, and when I saw it broadcast, the only edit left in was me enquiring of one of the students: "Have you brought your assignment?"

More excitingly, the Institute of Grocery Distribution (now known as the consultancy IGD) asked me to run part of its management training. This involved visiting the head offices and stores of the main supermarket retailers in the UK. I was asked to produce a training manual, including case studies, suitable for entry-level managers. This contained mostly theoretical topics such as leadership, communications and motivation; these topics were given a practical slant by my own experiences in the sector. I was still learning myself. At the well-appointed Tesco training centre, near Waltham Cross, the day was split between me and another trainer who conducted televised role-play sessions, turnabout with each group. At one meeting, I was explaining the art of selling bad news to an employee. The usual techniques were trotted out – the "sandwich", the "60-second" and so on. Many of the course members were graduates, and one scoffed loudly, saying that he could not see any of these methods working in a real-life situation. Excellent stuff in an effective training session. Unusually, the Derby store manager had slipped in to the room (head office quality control?). Before I could answer the student, the manager, obviously referencing Dr Blanchard's *The One Minute Manager* text said: "You're an assistant manager checking the canned goods section, and you find a shelf-filler in a hopeless mess – facings are back-to-front, upside-down, on their sides, in the wrong merchandise sections and everywhere else! Someone's left you a real task! Obviously, they haven't been trained that all cans have to be facing the customers so they can be read. I'll have to leave you to sort it out, I've got 10 phone calls to make. OK?" When teaching management subjects, I always wore a business suit with a shirt-matching silk handkerchief in the top pocket. One day, with a group at Morrison's head office in Bradford, a male student enquired why I had a pair of pink ladies' knickers in my pocket.

Although most of my research and consultancy was done when an employee of retail firms or when report writing for research houses, as described in the next chapter, I was consistently freelancing as individuals and businesses approached me. I was rarely out of work during my careers but was always glad to deal with a "fill-in" when it came along. Once, in Manchester, I was researching retail voluntary groups and their supply chains. I had arranged to meet the chief executive of such a group at 9am, and when we sat down in his office, he placed his watch on the desk in front of him and said, "I'll give you 10 minutes." Over an hour later, we were still talking, and I had enough data about his business for my needs. I had learned the old trick of getting informants to start talking about themselves ("how did you make this such a successful business?") Another time, I was approached by telephone by an independent retailer. I personally carried out research in the locality of his store and subsequently sent him a comprehensive report with proposals, enclosing a modest bill. He wrote back, saying that I had told him nothing new, and refused to pay. This must happen to many researchers. I noted it for the future and wrote off the debt. A Glasgow-based wholesaler wanted to expand in the Scottish central belt. I provided a map of food shop locations with their accessibility and relative values. I was paid. Again in Scotland, I was flattered to be approached by the late James Gulliver's organisation. His team asked me to assess a site in Stirling for one of their chain of new supermarkets. After careful analysis of the local competition, and of potential spending power, using government statistics, I vetoed the project in my report, citing the isolation of the site and the spread of more than adequate national competition, which targeted local socio-economic groups (this was in the 1970s). The report was ignored, and a new unit was opened to great success. The very brief that I had been given had not revealed that the new supermarket would be what was called in the trade a "hard discounter".

Sometimes, you have to laugh. In Keynsham, Somerset, I was trying to find the town hall to look at planning applications after receiving an enquiry from a Bristol-based retailer. I stopped the car and asked an old man where the town hall was. He reflected for a moment: "Well, we got two town 'alls now: one of them's being built, so there ain't no roof. Anyway, go straight on, and you'll see a road on the left (then very emphatically), don't go down there!" Further on, I spied a policeman who told me that I had just stopped outside the real town hall. Before this, I had gone into a newsagent for my *Financial Times*. The lady behind the counter, with cutting sarcasm, wished me "a lovely, lovely read". Collecting data often needs guile and confirmatory checks, particularly in the same company as the following illustrates. I was researching for a short article for "Retail Week" on the pattern of development retailers adopt when expanding their estates. With supermarkets it had been clear – Sainsbury filled up the South first, only venturing further north with the acquisition of a Coventry grocer, Morrison, after the Safeway take-over in the South. For me, at that time, it meant phoning companies. With the Burton Group (now part of online clothing retailer, Boohoo), I initially decided to go straight to the top and talk to Ralph

Halpern, the CEO (known to the press, unaccountably, as "Mister Five Times a Night"). His PA told me that he couldn't talk to me "as he was too busy making money", a phrase that was repeated in the conversation – and that was the end of that conversation. Unabashed, I redialled and spoke to Estates. A gentleman there said yes, he would send me a copy of the shop property register with all locations and addresses, which he did. This provided not only the "Retail Week" copy, but the substance of a report for the EIU "Retail Business".

Research often includes forecasting: what will a project be worth as an investment, and thus in cash value terms? These calculations, more often than not, are based on mathematical models. But the environments (economic, social, climate and so on) are non-linear, and the nearest to reality they arrive at is something like *Grand Theft Auto* the computer game, according to the economist John Kay. It is difficult to forecast pandemics, as recent experience shows, but events more closely related to human behaviour are easier to prognosticate. When I was working in the stock market, I learned that the fundamentals – supply and demand – are not the only influences on the economy. Sentiment – what people think and feel about things – is often more powerful. For example, during the Gulf War (1991), the Kuwaiti oilfields were put out of action by the Iraqis. In order to prevent the fall in oil supply to the market causing a price spike, Saudi Arabia, as the OPEC "swing producer", increased its own output to help stabilise the market. But market watchers and investors were worried that recrimination by external terrorist groups would sabotage Saudi production capacity; the result was a rise in petroleum prices. In my Chapter 8 story about estimating the size of the UK population in 2000 from a 1965 perspective, the same useless forecasting is illustrated. Now we look at a slightly more successful attempt.

Editor Edward McFadyen, introducing my regular financial column in *Retail & Distribution Management*, March/April 1988 wrote: "Just by way of being cheerful, our columnist is predicting a substantial down turn in consumer spending on durables and semi-durables over the next two or three years. He describes it as a 'purely qualitative assessment.'"

"Suddenly, economic forecasters of all shades are predicting a slowdown in the British economy in 1988. It is surely a sublime example of post facto reasoning when formerly bullish institutions downgrade their forecasts to accommodate changes in the real economy. What is the link with 'Black Monday'? No one seems to know. There are those who say that the severest fall in the securities market in half a century means little in real economy terms. Britain plc is enjoying its best boom since the early 1970s. Of course, we did suffer an equity market correction in 1974, followed by a downturn in the real economy, but today the economic fundamentals are quite different. They certainly are, and they look rather unhealthy.

Long wave theory has been out of fashion for five years and suffers from the old joke that the stock market has predicted the last four recessions out of three. The problem facing some city analysts is that they have consistently got their timing wrong. The fall in world equity markets was predicted variously for 1988, 1989 and even 1990. The immediate reason for the fall in equity prices was not computer trading programmes or even attempts at arbitrage between the NYSE and the Chicago futures exchanges, but a realisation among investors that the reverse yield gap between equities and bonds produced a classic switch situation. Investors moved out of low yielding equities into high yielding government securities. So why were equity prices so high?

Basically, too much money has been injected into shares. Too much money has been spent on property. Too much money is being spent on consumption rather on saving. The savings ratio in Britain has fallen to 5 per cent of income, the lowest since 1959. The money illusion has been created by inflation. The assets of which the economy is composed remain the same value, unless further capital is spent on upgrading them. Now we have three great piles of debt in the world economy – the sovereign, the corporate and the domestic.

We need a big resurgence in world trade to extinguish these debts. At present, there are no signs that this will occur. The US, huge engine of world trade, is slowly reducing its trade deficit, signalled by its historically weak dollar, by exporting as much as it can. There is less scope for European and British exports in this situation. Consequently, the future of the world economy, including Britain, suggests a downturn in trading activity. This must impact on our home economy in terms of earnings.

There is more than this, however. We face a saturation of home markets from the constant innovation accompanying the long boom and its after effects. Many product life cycles are in their decline stages, and we still have to see a wave of really new and innovative products in many sectors... expectations are already beginning to change, both in industry and among consumers. Thus the apparent reductions in purchases of consumer durables and semi-durables before Christmas. This column predicts a serious downturn in these product categories over the next two or three years. Prices will moderate as disinflation takes hold. This is a purely qualitative assessment, which distinguishes it from those of the business school and stockbroking fraternity where figures mean little more than their public relations value."

It was interesting to read *The Daily Telegraph* obituary (30 June 2020) of the very successful builder, Tony Pidgley: "When a customer sent Tony Pidgley a crate of champagne in 1988, he knew it was time for his housebuilding business to sell its stocks of homes and land. 'There was nothing magic in what I did' he said in his London barrow boy accent. 'It was smacking everybody in the eye. The customer sent me the champagne because he had made a £100,000 profit on a house he had bought from us only a few months earlier. This was not reality'. Pidgley turned his company's stock into cash at the top end of the market. By the time his rivals were scrambling to sell their land in 1991 in the midst of a recession, Berkeley (his company) was buying all it could at giveaway prices. Pidgley made millions and became the darling of the stock market."

This tale only further supports the contention that hands-on business people really do understand what's going on, as opposed to the academically inclined "experts". Take the case of Alan Budd, adviser to Mrs Thatcher and subsequent head of quango, the Office for Budget Responsibility. A friend who was CEO of a Shell subsidiary told me at the time that Alan, as a Shell advisor, had predicted that the recession would end in 1992 – shades of John Major's "green shoots" theory. It actually went on for another year. Sir Alan, as he now is, left George Osborne's Treasury "in a shambles" as head of OBR. (www.taxresearch.org.uk/ Google).

And remember that poor forecasting can affect lives as well as economic planning, particularly if it is executed incompetently. I am writing this on the morning after the screening on Channel 4 of an investigative programme by Antony Barnett on the second wave of Covid-19 (16 November 2020). Entitled "Lockdown Chaos – How The Government Lost Control". It showed, among other startling facts, how Test-and-Trace virus samples were physically handled in an unprofessional – nay casual – manner. Much of the work had been outsourced at staggering cost to Carillion-type firms and even, in one case, to a debt collecting agency. (Incidentally, until now I thought "lockdown" was about driving in LA.)

Chapter 11

WRITING

My first book was published in 1968, and the second four years later. Although I had worked as a "Saturday Boy" in an Edinburgh department store at the age of 16, retailing was just a job then. There was no connection with me applying to join the Littlewoods Store Group 10 years later on its management training course.

Retailing is a customer-facing activity and "very close to the till", as someone said. A huge number of interesting products are channelled through from producers to consumers. Your interpersonal skills – motivation and communication – are honed, along with leadership. In a well-structured and organised training scheme, you are actually in a sort of apprenticeship, learning by doing. This and the sparkle of retailing captured me at that time and provided an interesting and fruitful career. Don't listen to those who cry about the "death of the high street", there will always be "showrooms" alongside the growing online distribution systems (which themselves can provide fascinating jobs). At Littlewoods, I learned the rudiments of retailing – the importance of having advertised stock on display and in the right place, at the right time and in the right proportions, at the right price, with the right staff with the requisite skills – all with the necessary organisation and leadership.

At NCR, I was recruited to assess the suitability of retail sites for company clients. My work began before key models, such as the Huff and Lackshmanen-Hansen variants,based on Reilly's work were published. These spatial interaction models were fine for measuring the power of an individual shopping centre, but not for single shop units. Jack Cohen, the Tesco founder claimed to judge sites on "smell", by which he meant instinct. Clearly, a more rational approach, covering clustering, access, planning prospects and other positives need to be brought into the equation, as outlined in my first book, Retail Site Assessment. NCR , like IBM now calls itself a software and services group.

It was during my period working with John Menzies at its head office in Edinburgh that I landed the ultimate job for me. As recounted in Chapter 8, the company was on the cusp of a period of expansion, having just made an important acquisition. Human resources texts often laud the possibility that worker jobs can link stages where operators can also be involved in producing the final product – a difficult idea in this age of mass production. Because this was a completely new post for Menzies, I was able to write my own job specification. The stages of my job started with identifying towns and which of their shopping centres might accommodate a Menzies branch, taking into account potential spending power, level of competition and other factors, potential sites and their current footfall, planning status, store design and shopfitting, merchandising and final handover to field management. Obviously, this required liaison with internal departments such as finance, buying, HR and with outsourcers such as commercial estate agents, shopfitters and so on. The literary result of all this was *Retail Development*. Both books were published by Business Books, now part of the Informa Group, which focuses primarily on the exhibitions sector.

My third book was aimed at students who were studying retailing. The blurb explained that it was a simple and straightforward description of general retailing and its processes, along with the changes and challenges facing the sector in 1978, when it was published. It continued by announcing its suitability for students at HND level and for those studying other retailing qualifications. Unfortunately, in my enthusiasm for writing a more comprehensive, rather specialist book on the subject, I failed to canvass the potential market properly. Retailing only became a popular subject for academic studies during the 1980s when major brand development and international expansion by hundreds of retailers occurred. University departments, such as at Stirling and Oxford, were formed, along with the rise of retail consultancies such as Retail Intelligence. McDonald & Evans (soon to be part of Pearson) was the publisher. After two or three years, they wrote to ask, in view of falling sales, whether I would like to purchase the balance of the stock. One of my students, a Nigerian, told me that he could offload them profitably in Lagos, but I regretfully declined the offer. Help of a kind appeared in the shape of Paul Brittain, a lecturer at Nottingham-Trent. He taught retailing and had a retail background and asked me if he could co-author a sequel. My first thought was negative – why should I compromise my own hard work, particularly with someone I did not know? What were his motives? University lecturers were being encouraged more and more to carry out research. Oxbridge and some other Russell members were spending so much of their resources on research work that it could overshadow teaching, surely their main purpose. Also some well-received published work could lead to advancement. But then I thought of the royalties, and the book needed updating and could benefit with new and different input. Apart from that, as mentioned above, the retail sector was on a roll, with a consequent increase in staffing and thus the need for more academic courses. So I gladly welcomed Paul into an informal partnership. The result was brilliant: the book went into five editions, with its last in 2004. This was very much due to Paul, who brought a great deal of relative text in the form of marketing applied to retail operations. In turn, I boosted the strategic aspects of retail planning, alongside Paul's tactical input. Unfortunately, since the last edition was published, we have suffered a financial crisis, a pandemic and the impact of tech. If the publisher had permitted a sixth edition, I had planned to add a new chapter on the now vital corporate elements of ESG (environment, social, governance).

Kogan Page, a business publisher, was developing a range of "Working for Yourself" books, aimed at people who were either thinking about starting a small business or seeking advice for an existing one. I approached them with a proposal, and in due course, *Running Your Own Shop* appeared in 1985, with a second edition three years later. In the early 1990s, I was contacted by the author of a similar book which had been published in 1972. He complained that I had used material from it, notably a calendar of retail promotional occasions, without acknowledgement. He was, of course, quite right to challenge this breach of copyright. I apologised and freely admitted my clumsy oversight. His attitude seemed to become friendlier, and he invited me to a meeting in a London hotel. Here he invited me to talk on a course he was organising for East Anglian retail gas managers. I accepted and carried out the engagement at the board headquarters. I was not paid for this but recognised that it was some compensation for my oversight. Latterly, he persuaded my publisher Kogan Page to extract a considerable sum of money in further retribution. I did not object to this but was concerned that my publisher had been involved. Obviously, the matter could have ended up in court, with considerably more to pay, but I would have been happier to have reached an equable outcome with the author personally. Now, years later, I see it as part of the authors' experience; it is useful, for instance, to tell this story to students who are writing their theses that plagiarism could lead to unforeseen consequences.

My own MA thesis was published in the *Handbook of Retailing*, edited by Alan West and published by Gower in 1988. A further piece on retail mergers appeared in *The Changing Face of British Retailing*, edited by Edward McFadyen and published by Newman Books in 1987. Edward is mentioned previously as part of our lengthy and happy association when I was the financial correspondent of *Retail & Distribution Management* journal. I had a similar link with Evelyn Clerk, editor of *Retail Business*, the former Economist Intelligence Unit publication. I was also a contributor to Euromonitor Retail and Distribution Surveys and to a similar Mintel series – I really blew it with this research house when it commissioned me to write a report in the 1990s on personal electronic devices and their distribution. I agreed, thinking more about the fee than the subject – retailing in the sector was easy, but I eventually realised that my expertise on the devices was minimal. That was the end of my time with Mintel. It's tough to take on self-knowledge in your 50s.

Writing is one of my most enjoyable hobbies, and this is why I am engaged in a memoir in my retirement. My books have been translated into Mandarin, Greek, Czech and Polish; there is even a very low-cost edition of *Retailing: An Introduction* in English for the Indian market. A confession – although I love writing about retail, I dislike teaching it. Perhaps this is because my presentation lacks student involvement, and they complain to the head teacher – this happened to me at Regent's College when I was sacked (so was the head teacher). I should have appeared in an old Sainsbury managers' calico jacket in front of a counter loaded with attractive goodies, adopting a roistering approach to the saleability of aforesaid items and pleading for queries from the assembled company. Slightly more seriously, the mention of hobbies leads into my entry in the Writers' Directory, which is totally boring on that subject, but on a trip between Chattanooga and Atlanta a couple of years ago, there was a revelation. A young lady who I had become friendly with was obviously trying to find out more about me. She was googling fiercely and suddenly remarked that I liked touring the States, fine dining and "being silly". I countered that the Amazon entry was accurate, but that it had been culled from my profile in "Who's Who in the World". Further,

Amazon had translated one of the companies – NCR – that I had worked for as North Carolina; my arrival in the United States had been advanced by 20 years.

It must be said in conclusion to this chapter on my writing that the first two books lacked any insight into the vital human aspect of retailing. This was a reflection of the sector in the 1960s and 1970s, before its expansion and modernisation. Later editions of my last book, *Retailing: An Introduction*, outlined the failings of management in this and other areas of their responsibility. For example, from the 5th Edition: "The sector is more product than people focused, a situation not helped by the centralisation multiples have imposed on their structures. Because it is operationally biased, it is more short-termist and tends to lack strategic vision. Traditionally, the industry is seen as a young persons' game, offering 'holiday' jobs in low-paid, low-skill occupations with few prospects of promotion and personal development; staff turnover, as a result, averages 30 per cent. Strategically, retail has been criticised: John Richards (for many years one of the city's leading analysts and an ex-colleague) has followed such well-known retailers as Ralph Halpern, Gerald Ratner and George Davies (he could now include Philip Green). He said he has seen a recurrent pattern of retail entrepreneurs 'creating something wonderful that they subsequently smash to bits.'"

My own career migration to the business education sector alerted me to the full importance of people in organisations – a transition that introduced me to modern theory and formed the basis of this book's title. For instance, teaching of marketing has moved from the basic product-based 4Ps model to concepts such as societal marketing and customer orientation and relationship development. If I had been more aware of this at Philips, when I was asked to prepare plans for staff shops to be converted to self-service, I would have invited potential users to advise me on what they wanted. A significant book which helps re-align thinking in this century was Daniel Goleman's *Emotional Intelligence*. Organisationally, a key book on personal interactions is Gillian Tett's *The Silo Effect*.

Chapter 12

MUSINGS

Many people want to retire early, perhaps in their 50's or even before. They may have become multi-millionaires, which seems to have been made much easier in this century. Or they are releasing themselves from the drudgery of a meaningless occupation. Or from a highly stressful job, where pressure is mercilessly dialled up by an evil manager. And this in the age where "60 is the new 40". But what is to follow? Many years of loneliness and boredom, followed by a drift into mental illness? Clearly, that is not the end that one wants to contemplate. That is why many more are becoming self-employed, and the gig economy is being born. Unfortunately, Covid-19 has begun, if not to destroy this new sector, at least to shake it up.

Owen Palmer and I, as teaching colleagues at GSM, made a pact that we would try to keep on working there until we were at least 75 years old. You can do this in teaching – Ben Elton's grandfather was still lecturing at Tel Aviv University until his mid-nineties. Both Owen and I achieved our goal, but sadly he died at just over 80. Until 2019, at the age of 83, I was still lecturing at

GSM, but after 27 years serving there, it all ended when the Greenwich School of Management went into liquidation (full story in Chapter 9). My first intention was to keep on working. With my experience, I thought of becoming a non-executive director, particularly as I had been the owner of a small private company for 20 years. Unusually, I did not do any specific research in this area. I knew that it was a popular option for retired managers and was also controversial. There had been so many corporate disasters in recent years, and non-execs on their boards had often been accused of blindness to the governance competence of the executive directors. Outsourcers, such as the Big Four accountancy firms, all international giants, had, in a number of cases, failed to identify flawed client accounting; this had resulted in their being fined by the FCA. The Financial Conduct Authority itself had faced criticism for weak responses to allegations, and because its own governance had been influenced by the presence of ex-partners of the Big Four co-opted to its board. The FCA, as a result, is being reshaped.

All that said, I contacted a northern firm that offered training for would-be non-executive directors. All communication was carried out online and, on request, I paid £600, apparently as a joining fee. Soon after, I was asked for a further £1,500, which seemed to be training course fees. I baulked at this, as I had just lost my job. (I had asked GSM for an ex gratia payment to compensate for a pension-free 27 years, but this was refused.) Then I was assailed by emails from a variety of names, which suggested quite a large organisation. In the end, I wrote off the £600 and indicated that I did not want further contact. Eventually, this happened, except that many months later, I appeared to be receiving invitations to more courses. What I should have done was to get on to the *Financial Times*, which I have been reading for 60 years. It provided me with information on its own long-established courses for would-be non-executive directors at acceptable prices. By this time, I had virtually abandoned the idea, at least for the time being. An easier course might be to pursue my disrupted career in HE. As a start, I engaged with online agents such as Indeed and Reed.

Indeed operates under many sub-brands, with some focusing on particular geographical areas. I was happy for them to search Kent, Surrey, Sussex and South East London – all within an hour's drive. This went on for over a year, during which I was offered two interviews, one of which produced a few hours teaching at a Chatham Grammar School and a mock exam marking for around 50 students; this was quite enjoyable, but not very satisfying. My problem was that as someone who had spent many years lecturing at Higher Education levels 5–7, adjusting to even FE levels was difficult – but most of the vacancies offered were on Secondary courses. The gap between running an EMBA module on strategic management to a business manager group and an elementary book-keeping class for 12-year-olds was almost impossible to bridge. I created a school-type CV, but this only prompted school job specifications aimed at me that emphasised, often in capitals, that they were looking for teachers not lecturers. Some friends have suggested to me that there is little difference, but none of them had been at the sharp end of education. The difference is one of style and attitude. Because I have had the happy experience of not only being paid for but thoroughly enjoying every single job I have done, I felt that at this stage in my life, I wanted to continue on the same path.

Clearly, one enjoyable occupation for me has been writing, as described in Chapter 10. But getting published is becoming more difficult, particularly for first-timers. Fifty years ago, when I was working for bookseller John Menzies, new books published were probably a 10th of the volumes today. Covid-19 has apparently led to many more manuscripts arriving at publishing houses. From the publication of my first book in 1968, until 15 years ago, I was able to approach publishers directly with my book proposals and have them adopted. Business Books organised a print run of 2,500 copies, of which half were bound; the balance was probably pulped and, when regenerated, may even have formed the basis of the second of my books. This publisher may not have made a profit on these titles. In those days, most publishers were small and probably just as interested in their craft as a fulfilling vocational skill as the financial side. Today, large groups dominate the sector. As I type this, *The Times* business section on the desk beside me tells me that the giant German Bertelsmann media group is to take over Simon & Schuster. These businesses are very commercial and profit-focused and, in my view, less friendly towards the people who help them make their profits. I have now given up direct contacts with publishers, largely because if they respond at all, they refer you to literary agents. I had an agent 50 years ago, and he was useless. Of course, I have taken publisher advice – Bloomsbury sent me a nice, personal letter, the company signed the Hachette missive. But the agents are not much better; they clearly lack refined judgement, evidenced by the constant stream of bestsellers they fail to spot when an MS lands on a commissioning editor's desk. How about a bit more properly directed marketing research? So, the default position seems to be self-publishing.

The most worrying result of losing my job at GSM was a debt of nearly £30,000. This was comprised of outstanding balances on four credit cards and an overdraft of £2,500 on my personal bank account; I had just cleared an overdraft of £5,000 on my company account. Fortunately, I had no other outstanding debts; my house mortgage had been extinguished through an equity withdrawal (discussed later). I decided almost immediately that I would seek advice from the Citizens' Advice Bureau. I remembered that I had sought help from CAB at Marylebone Town Hall when I first moved to London; it was very helpful over an accommodation matter. Before this, I had consulted my sons, who had both been victims of the unsolicited credit card scams at the end of the century. They variously suggested the StepChange Debt Charity and even an Individual Voluntary Agreement (IVAs are discussed later). Before sending my last payments to creditors, I explained my financial position. Some banks told me that they could do nothing until I defaulted, but this was one way of further establishing trust between the parties. It is essential to record all communications at this point; banks routinely do this with phone, text and email messages, and copies of letters should be kept by debtors.

The staff at the Edenbridge branch of CAB could not be praised enough for their friendly attitude, professional approach and diligence in helping you. They produced income and expenses statements and contacted all my creditors, negotiating mutually agreed repayments for all the cards and the overdraft. The staff, particularly Kate, interviewed me several times over many months and advised me on many ways I could reduce my outgoings. The arrangement agreed is not supported by the law, and this emphasises the importance of trust in the relationship. On the other hand, an IVA is a formal and legally binding agreement between you and your creditors to pay back your debts, usually over five years. It needs help from an insolvency practitioner – a lawyer or accountant – who charges £5,000 for the service. Debts could be quickly paid through equity withdrawal. These schemes allow older, freehold owners to borrow against the current value of their houses. The advantages of this are that instead of paying monthly, the interest charges are rolled up, added to the principle of the loan and only paid back when the house is sold, or the owner goes into care or dies. The problems may involve high compound interest and the costs of ending a contract early. This was illustrated in a *Times* money report: "£750k equity release broke our hearts" by David Byers, 28 November 2020. In this case, the beneficiary received less than 20 per cent of the final value. In my own case, a firm called Age Partnership sends me letters fortnightly suggesting that I could extract 54 per cent of my house equity through one of the many vendors currently offering these lifetime mortgages. I have told them several times that I am happy with my current arrangements; so are my three children who were informed of them at the outset.

I mention very early on my interest in cars and motoring. As a preamble to this side of my life, I now include a short story, based on real events experienced 50 years ago. (It was originally a competition entry and is unpublished.)

THE BRIDGE

The Blue Boar teemed with lunchers. Heavy rain had chased many off the M1 into the relative security of the Watford Gap Service Area. I walked out of the cafeteria, passing at the cigarette machine to gratify one of my baser instincts.

"Excuse me, sir, are you going North?" A stockily-built man in his early 30s wearing a coloured windcheater had spoken to me.

"Sure, I'm actually turning off south down the M5 in Birmingham, but I can certainly take you that far."

To my surprise, he nodded. "Are you going past the service place at the top of the M5?"

"Yes – that's Frankley, isn't it?"

"The reason I'm asking, sir, is that the fish wagons stop there at 3 o'clock on their way up to Aberdeen. That's where I'm going. I can cross over the bridge there to get to the Northbound," he added.

"Just let me go to the gents', and I'll be with you," I countered, admiring the effrontery of someone who had asked for a lift inside the service area building.

The rain had eased to a light drizzle as I steered the Mercedes through the exit road to the motorway. Two bedraggled students peered through moisture-flecked spectacles at us as we accelerated past them.

My new companion snorted softly: "You didn't mind me asking you inside the place, did you?" He extended his hand and leaned back against the door pillar. "I may be wrong, but I can't see any point in standing outside in this lousy weather."

"Seems sensible," I agreed, "but you're the first person to have approached me like that, and I've been up and down this motorway most weeks for the past year."

Again he apologised, obliquely.

We were moving quickly now. I overtook, with some elation, a BMW, sensing that he would soon be on my tail, pitting his not inconsiderable engine power against mine.

"First time I've been on a motorway; if you ask me, it's like playing dodgems for real." He grinned.

"Mm. Can be sticky up to Luton, particularly in this sort of weather and with a few nasty wagon drivers." I smiled back.

My passenger lapsed into silence.

We were now passing the European-looking Chelmsley Wood housing estate, to the east of Birmingham. "Do you know Aberdeen?" He asked suddenly.

"Fairly well. It's a fine city, and with this oil boom, well, it could become the Hamburg of Scotland. Are you going up there for work? I believe they are crying out for labour. Particularly outside the city where they're building the rigs, the houses, and things to go with them."

"You think that there are chances up there, do you?" He asked eagerly.

"Sure. Depends on your line of business. What do you do?"

He didn't answer immediately. I saw out of the corner of my eye his hands, wagging pendulously. "Look," he blurted, at last, "I'm sick and tired telling lies about it. Once you've told one lie, you've got to build a big story, and I just can't do that." He faced me. "I've been inside, see. Just come out."

A Spanish juggernaut loaded, for all I knew, with castanets, was pulling out inexorably, directly in front of me. There was a resigned silence in the car. I tucked the Merc safely in front of the Spaniard and reduced speed. "I see."

"I slept rough near Hemel last night, 'cause I didn't have a cent," he went on quickly, "and I knocked off these fags from a machine. I got seven pence change and bought a cup of tea; that was breakfast," he finished, with a slight touch of bravado in his voice.

"I've often wondered how you cheat cigarette machines," I murmured.

He proceeded to tell me in some detail how this was done. "Stolen fags seem to taste better." Mine was beginning to burn my palate.

He started again. "I'm a locksmith by trade, but I wasn't done for anything like that. No." He enunciated the words like a news reader: "Conspiracy to pervert the course of justice. I bribed a couple of witnesses to a bank robbery and got sent down for the same as the thieves themselves. Eight years. It was fair, though."

"Does crime pay?" I was talking in clichés.

"No. I want to go straight. Prison's for the mugs. Trouble is, I haven't any money, because you have to have a permanent address to go to when you come out. Most prisoners do, but I don't have no one to go to. I'm due £170, if I claim it in the next few days, but the trouble is they don't wanna know you if you're an ex-prisoner, looking for work without a permanent address."

"Chicken and egg," I grunted, without thinking.

"Yeah."

We were climbing over the Gravelly Hill interchange. "This is the famous 'Spaghetti Junction'," I told him.

"Blimey, this place wasn't even built when I was inside. You read about things like this and see it on television, but when you come out, it's all kind of different. If you only got the media, you get a funny picture of everything."

"What is being in prison really like?"

His hands waved again. "Basically, it gets your mind. If you didn't let go sometimes, your mind'd go. I was in for 10, through losing two year's remission. The screws had these new locks put on the doors, which they said were completely unbustable and foolproof. I got hold of some Bostik, melted it down and poured it into the locks and buggered the lot. Cost them thousands!" He went on: "But with this technology thing, this country's fantastic! Saw this American car bloke on TV the other night, talking about Rolls-Royce. He said what country in the world could have a company go bust and next day announce a new model? You gotta hand it to them." He laughed delightedly.

The Mercedes was moving past the Dudley exit. "See this bruise?" He showed me a blue mark on his temple. "That was a police inspector did that. I've only been out for four days, and I went off down to Brighton, to see if I could contact one of the blokes who'd been done with me. Police picked me up and done me over. I was wearing a blue shirt at the time, and the blood from my nose was all over it. The inspector tosses me a red shirt in the station and says the blood shouldn't show the next time. Bloody sense of humour."

We were turning into the Southbound Frankley Services Area, and Elton John's cover of *Lucy in the Sky* was playing on the car radio. He pointed at it. "You know when the Beatles brought out their *Sergeant Pepper* album, some bloke tells the BBC that there's a drug song on it. They listen to all the tracks and ban *A Day in the Life*. Marvellous!" He snorted derisively.

"Well, here we are," I opined.

He reached for his jacket, and as he got out of the car, I opened my wallet and gave him a pound. "Thanks for the entertainment."

His face changed from blankness to delight. "Thanks," he muttered as he turned towards the car park. It had stopped raining.

I accelerated towards the South, but in the rear-view mirror I could see him gesticulating – or waving farewell? But the rear-view mirror also revealed that Frankley Services had no overbridge. By now, the Merc was doing the ton. End of the story.

One of the best perks of employment, certainly in my day, was being allocated a company car. But for me, it was a necessity as someone who had to drive all over Britain and Ireland to view retail sites. In Dublin, I would hire a vehicle ay the airport; flights to Dundee from City Airport were not always convenient, so I would drive north from Edinburgh. Apart from that, public transport from my West Kent town, which had lost its rail link with the Beeching clear out, was difficult. My first car was a Morris Minor, which I bought in North London; after a few weeks, the engine went (the car had probably been "clocked"). A replacement engine cost less than £50 in the early 1960s. In those days, cars, particularly British ones, rarely seemed to reach a mileage of more than 70,000. For years, Honest John in his *Telegraph* column had alleged that manufacturers expect only a seven-year life for the average car. But with many vehicles today easily doubling that, this estimate may need revising. Much of the improvement has been due to German and East Asian progress in design, of course. However, over the years, HJ has provided many useful hints and tips on better driving; block changing and cadence braking were two ideas new to me. Incidentally, has anyone noticed that lorry tail notices have been reduced to warnings to cyclists? Two of my favourites were the Scottish "Dinnae hug me, a'm going steady" and the sterner German: "Unter Sie Gehen!"

As to the marques provided at my level in the various companies I served, they were Minis at Sainsbury, Ford Cortinas at British Bakeries, a Morris 1300 at Menzies (at one point in the fast lane of the M1, my front nearside tyre burst. Instead of somersaulting, I managed to steer the car to the hard shoulder, thanks to the awareness of the vehicles around me). At Philips, we were allowed Vauxhall Victor 1800s; in those days, many companies insourced transport and when I exchanged my first car, the manager opened the bonnet and allegedly declared that "the engine fell apart". Certainly, I had whacked it going up and down the M1/M6, reaching 114 mph on the clock, just once. With the need for two cars in the family, company cars were possible for me until 1975, but only to 1969 for Liz. After a bit, we opted for German, Japanese and French vehicles. Then, of course, the three children obtained their own cars; fortunately this coincided, roughly, with their desertion of the household.

Q. What excuse do some motorists give if their car is repossessed?

A. It was stolen by thieves who managed, by electronic trickery, to open, start and drive it away from my house!

Is this really possible? Let us say that you have lost the single key you had to lock and start your car; the vehicle is standing in a public car park (usually, quality cars are provided with three keys at sale, and others are available at the manufacturers). To retrieve the car, first of all the key configuration is measured by injecting sensing fluid into the lock. This data is scanned on a laptop attached to a 3D printer, which converts blanks into keys that will fit the lock; the vehicle can now be opened. But it cannot be started; this requires that the engine ignition system be removed and its code scanned and incorporated in the key, through the laptop. Then the car can be opened and the engine started for a drive away. Simple? Only if you have the right software and skills to use it.

Incidentally, some alert readers may have been puzzled by my temporary friend's penultimate giggle in the short story above. (The dialogue is genuine and authentically recorded, but I only noticed the disparity when writing up for this memoir.) His comments about Rolls-Royce are nonsense; he refers to the collapse of the Aeroengine Division and its reincarnation as Rolls-Royce (1971) by accountant Rupert Nicholson of what is now KPMG. In addition to the fees, the company gave him a Rolls-Royce to thank him personally. Nicholson was the father of my good friend "Nick" Nicholson.

FROM PRACTICE TO THEORY

I first met Nick through Liz, who worked with Sally, his fiancée, at Van den Bergh. He was studying to be an architect and finally became very successful with his own practice in Tunbridge Wells; latterly his many commissions spread as widely as Dundee to Bordeaux. Living in Central London, my flatmates threw many parties in that social 1960s environment. One of the things we enjoyed about the new Bond films was the copious consumption of cocktails. We decided to organise a party themed on the martini, with the addition of sherry, which was still popular then. Unfortunately, we had no clue about making the New York style of the drink; the inevitable result was a super surfeit of gin in the mixture. The plan was that after the party, we would all go to an Italian restaurant round the corner in Marylebone High Street. On meeting the fresh air outside the flat, Nick fell on his face. Consequently, he and Sally did not make supper with us and instead made off to her flat in Tedworth Square. (She later confessed that this was the first time she had slept with him.) Nick, for his part, remembered being hit by something like a scaffolding pole. Over the next years, our two families shared much, such as holidays in Malta, Portugal, Scotland and elsewhere. Nick was a good golfer, and in trips to Le Touquet proved a staunch partner, particularly as we two were the loudest snorers on the tours. Colin Baker, another member of the Octagons, was an accountant; he had started working for large city firms, but latterly set up his own profitable business. Married to Christine, they lived for many years in Halstead, Kent. Like many of us, he was a keen rugby fan and also played with two or three of us for Sevenoaks RFC. One of the big annual occasions was the Twickenham Sevens Tournament. We usually arrived around midday and left at six; this was a lot of drinking time, and Colin – a big man – usually offered to drive us home, on the basis that he "had drunk only five pints". As the century ended, the atmosphere at this event changed, in our view, for the worst. It may have been a coincidence, but when an East End club fielded a team, we suddenly saw 14-year-old lads in fisticuff mode. Moreover, the Mexican Wave became an approbation feature; this had the effect of drowning everyone with liquids as spectators waved their clutched cans. So the old fogeys switched to watching the normal Rugby Union Internationals, rotating in our respective houses. On one occasion, we drove to Colin Robert's farm at Bala, North Wales. On the way, someone remembered that Colin did not have Sky. No problem, Colin took us to the local hotel to watch the England-Wales contest. The former won by a landslide, and we began to look around the huge Welsh fan base surrounding us, the only English there. No need to worry, the locals took it all sportingly as rugby fans inevitably do in Britain. Liz and I met the Mackays when we moved to Edinburgh in 1968. Both Hugh and Christine became firm friends over many years. Hugh, as an IBM executive, moved from Scotland to London and then to Athens and Paris and back to London. We were lucky enough to be able to stay with them in their overseas postings. Hugh had formidable intellect and a glorious sense of humour. We shared many dinner and drinks parties with them, and the four of us had a wonderful holiday in Marrakesh, meeting mutual friends, Noel and Jane Reid, at one of the city's marvellous hotels. Both Liz and I enjoyed the traditional bargaining in the souk, off the city's massive square, but the Mackay's did not. Fortunately, the Moroccan Government runs shops with conventional pricing for non-gamers.

A family with which we became so friendly that, at one stage, we joked that we should merge! The Haywards are still in this category. Laurence and Gill have produced six offspring, equally divided gender-wise. Two of my own children and myself still meet up with then, regularly, after nearly 50 years. The Hayward family lived in a string of large houses in Sevenoaks, Wadhurst and Elgin. They also hosted six spectacular weddings, all but one held in the spacious grounds of their Scottish mansion. This was once the home of the Macallan family, producers of what some claim as the finest single malt whisky (others in the Western Isles may dispute the Speyside claim). The family business, now run by the two elder sons, Austin and Matthew, is wine importing. Simon and I see them both regularly for lunch, along with long-standing friend Tim Broadhurst, an ex-reassurance director in the city, who was also an Octagon member – the only one to achieve a hole-in-one in the 20 years of the society's existence. The Cox and Hayward families holidayed together, notably in Portugal, often accompanied by the family of Roger and June Andrew (sadly, June died in 2020). All the villa pools, filled with all the boys from the three families, rang with shouts of "Marco!" as they played their favourite game. I never understood it.

Nick, Colin, Hugh and Laurence also sadly passed away over the last 20 years. All are sorely missed but will be remembered with love by all who knew them.

Barrie and Angela Hallett have been friends of the family for over 40 years. Until a few years ago, they lived in a converted oast in the neighbouring village of Brasted; now the couple live in a splendid cottage on Wembury Bay, South Devon, with sailing access to the Channel. Barry was senior partner in a city quantity surveying practice and latterly became a property developer, notably in Westerham. He inaugurated a dining club for Sunday evenings, with mutual friends such as Mike Breen and Tim Coles. As a family, we often stayed at his cottages in Cornwall (Ange's native county), particularly at Delicious Mousehole.

Peter and Carolyn Scoble, again very long friends, live near Ticehurst. Peter was a keen member of our Octagons Golf Society and retired as senior partner of Boodle Hatfield, Princess Diana's solicitor. He prided himself, he once confided to me, as being a key non-PC shaker-up in the venerable firm. A sentiment close to my own heart. After our disastrous move back from Edinburgh, the Scobles looked after us at their Badger's Mount house until we could buy new furniture.

Brandon Hayward is cousin to the other Haywards and is also in the wine trade. We meet with other friends, like David Roberts, an architect, and Mickey Barnard, a retired accountant, in local pubs – the latter two were also Octagon members. Brandon is a member of the HAC, and he has invited these friends to lunches and ceremonial dinners at Armoury House (my earlier association with the company is described in Chapter 6).

Turning to the "fairer sex" (are we still allowed to use this descriptor in the "cancel" context?), I first met Giannina in 2008, where she joined GSM as a mature student. The daughter of a Sardinian architect, she is the only person I know who has attended four universities: Turin, Avignon, Plymouth (GSM franchise) and Westminster. While in Europe, she was an Erasmus student. She took a BSc at Plymouth and an MA at the latter. A woman of taste, she had previously worked for Harley Davidson and Vertu. After graduating, she was a translator for law courts in London and the home counties, mostly representing Italian defendants; she is also fluent in French and English. Several senior female lecturers at GSM have claimed me as their mentor, and I was surprised when they made their admission; I suppose it was better not to know. I had unknowingly been in this role, but only in teaching. At CMMS at Wandsworth, I advised a young Jamaican woman, keen to become a confident lecturer, to try to supplement the definition of an item with two or three alternatives – important in multinational classes. I was more of a friendly counsellor to Giannina, particularly after her graduation. Advice on the use of English was important; an extreme example was her pronunciation of Canary Wharf – Cannery Wharf seemed more San Francisco docks than the London equivalent.

Graduations were held at the University of Plymouth campus. Students liked travelling there and taking part in the ceremony, along with photo opportunities on Plymouth Hoe.

A huge marquee was resplendent with food courts and bars, and it was always a grand day out without rain. As mentioned in Chapter 8, the academic visits there were always fruitful, and the university and its staff lived up to its reputation as one of the very best of the new universities. At Greenwich, Giannina was part of a clique of very intelligent student friends from several European, Asian and African countries, notably Alan West, who asked me for special economics tutoring, as did several other keen students.

She was a strong-minded woman who did not suffer fools gladly. Of the many books I gave her were, notably, George Orwell novels, Kingsley Amis on literary style and Dylan Thomas's collected poems; my own *How to run your own shop* was greeted as "patronising". In defence, my wife's cousin Trevor Beer, an ex-Harrods' menswear buyer, and his daughters, who own an upscale clothing store in Bramhall, patronised by Northern footballers and their WAGs told me "it was easy to read!" Giannina herself gave me two books by one of her favourite writers, Beppe Severgnini, and a copy of the classic *Pereira Maintains* by Antonio Tabucchi. She was also interested in British history. At Hever Castle, we were taken on a private tour of the state apartments where Henry VIII and Anne Boleyn lived from time to time. We also visited Penshurst Place, which the King used as a hunting lodge and is associated with his fourth wife, Anne of Cleves. Today, it is used for local events. Liz and I were invited by Chairman John Durtnell to the 400th anniversary of the eponymous builder, which has created prestigious work for the British Museum and RMA Sandhurst. At a wedding hosted by Jim and Sue Brown and run by Liz, on a scorching hot day at the venue, the cake made by a local cake-maker started to collapse; my wife, as a guest, jumped up and just managed to save it.

Another great interest that we shared was music, and we attended concerts in the Albert and Wigmore Halls and several London churches, especially for choral music, which she was very fond of. Her favourite newspaper was *The Guardian*, and I occasionally bought her a copy. One day, I stopped my BMW in a West Norwood garage forecourt and rushed over to a newsagent. When I returned, I found that my car had been clamped. The garage owner demanded £200 for illegal parking. There was no alternative but to extract the cash from the conveniently sited ATM. When I met Giannina a little later, she joked that this was the most expensive paper she had ever had. *The Guardian* made up for this later, when she found an article that suggested that students could obtain reduced rent if they agreed to act as a part-time carer. This happenstance resulted in her move from modest Tulse Hill to grand Hampstead. She joined the household of Barbara Law, whose two children lived separately but looked in as required. She was a widow in her late 80s, previously married to John, the leader of one of the London symphony orchestras and also a talented painter of cityscapes. Barbara herself was also an amateur artist, having produced portraits of the many orchestral conductors she and her husband had encountered as his orchestra travelled the world. She and Giannina immediately gelled. Barbara was a character who would sing Cockney songs like *My old Man* and *The Lambeth Walk* and joke about her future in couplets, which rhymed "coughing " with "coffin". She suffered from Alzheimer's disease and died around her 90th birthday. The funeral was held at Golders Green Crematorium. Giannina and I touched the casket as we left for the wake; this was held in The Old Bush and Bull pub, one of the subjects of Barbara's ditties. Just to illustrate Giannina's sensitivity, I append a very appropriate John Donne poem she sent me some years ago; it is still on the notice board in my study at home.

THE AUTUMNAL

No spring, nor summer beauty hath such grace
  As I have seen in one autumnal face;
Young beauties force our love, and that's a rape;
  This doth but counsel, yet you cannot scape.
If 'twere a shame to love, here 'twere no shame;
  Affections here take reverence's name.
Were her first years the Golden Age? That's true.
  But now they're gold, and ever new.
That was her torrid and inflaming time;
  This is her tolerable tropic clime.
Fair eyes; who asks more heat than comes from hence,
  He in a fever wishes pestilence.
Call not these wrinkles graves; if graves they were,
  They were Love's graves for else he is nowhere.
Yet lies not Love dead here, but here doth sit,
  Vow'd to this trench, like an anchorite.
And here, till hers, which must be his death, come.
  He doth not dig a grave, but build a tomb.
Here dwells he; though he sojourn everywhere,
  In progress, yet his standing house is here;
Here, where still evening is, not noon or night;
  Where no voluptuousness, yet all delight.
In all her words, unto all bearers fit,
  You may at revels, you at council sit.
This is love's timber; youth his underwood;
  There he, as wine in June, enrages blood;
Which then comes season ablest when our taste

And appetite to other things is past.
Xerxes' strange Lydian love, the platane tree,
Was loved for age, none being as large as she;
Or else because, being young, nature did bless
Her youth with age's glory, barrenness.
If we love things long sought, age is a thing
Which we are fifty years in compassing;
If transitory things, which soon decay,
Age must be loveliest at the latest day.
But name not winter faces, whose skin's slack,
Lank as an unthrift's purse, but a soul's sack;
Whose eyes seek light within, for all here's shade;
Whose mouths are holes, rather worn out , than made;
Whose every tooth to a several place is gone,
To vex their souls at resurrection;
Name not these living death-heads unto me.
For these, not ancient, but antique be.
I hate extremes; yet I would rather stay
With tombs than cradles, to wear out a day.
Since such love's motion natural is, may still
My love descend, and journey down the hill,
Not panting after growing beauties; so
I shall ebb out with them who homeward go.

Like many retirees, I have taken up walking as a pastime and a fitness option. Not the professional-looking Nordic style using hand-held poles like skiers, which have the extra advantage of upper body workouts, but short walks around the Kent-Surrey border. I walk with Rosemary, and we first met through WADS, our local amdram group. She had forgotten about this when we happened to bump into each other outside the local Co-op one day. When I finally found her house after she invited me in for a drink – at the third attempt on foot – I gave her a copy of a photograph of the cast of a farce we had both been in during the 1970s. At this time, her husband Michael had been the family GP. Her father had won an MC during the Great War. Unhappily, her mother had decamped from their Iver Heath home to join a music master at Eton. Rosemary joined the WRNS after World War Two and later became a professional speech trainer. Of Scottish descent, she is directly related to Lord Cockburn, the eminent judge. Very sadly, Rosemary Pearson passed away on Thursday, 8th. April, 2021. As a close friend, I shall miss her, and our walks together with enormous sorrow.

Most people who live in our area, which is very agricultural and with large swathes of woodland, see it as exceedingly beautiful. We can find extensive walks south of the town beside the two main roads, Hosey Hill and Goodley Stock. The former leads us towards Edenbridge, not only to the banks of the River Eden but to hamlets like Marsh Green and to major destinations already mentioned – Chartwell, Hever and Penshurst – not to mention Chiddingstone, with its castle and Chiding Stone (where the Jarrold Short Walks guide mollifyingly explains that "grievances were aired... and offenders chided"). Goodley Stock takes us to Limpsfield Chart and Crockhamhill Common and Village. Just outside of the latter, near Hurst Farm and on the hill, Rosemary and I found an apparently ancient semi-circle of stones; locals told us that it was a Victorian folly (on the other hand, the story could have been that it had been created on instructions by the Wizard of Penge by his followers. My friend Bill McLean had invented the character and wanted to write an opera with its name; one of Bill's other constructs was a 1960s band called Formica Armpit, which might accompany part of the mooted opera). To the north, we not only have Pilgrims' Way but the North Downs Way and Titsey Place and Park (both in Surrey). Over the other side of the A25 is the windmill at Outwood. To the east are the villages of Brasted, where the White Hart pub entertained fighter pilots from Biggin Hill during World War Two (the original board upon which the airmen signed their names has long since become a collectors' item), and Sundridge, where just beyond the church is a copse of Spanish Chestnut trees, planted in 1588 in commemoration of the victory over the Spanish Armada. Further on, Sevenoaks is surrounded by parks such as Knole, with its famous house and deer park, and many woods and forests flanking the A21, which splits from the M25 London Orbital Motorway and the A25 which runs through Westerham. Interestingly, here the road "pinches" at each end of the central green and market place; a similar narrowing at the top of London Road (the bane of bus drivers) was clearly designed as a defensive measure for any attacks on the town at the time of its 13th century build. A quite different slant on the town, according to a *Daily Telegraph* survey some years ago, is that Sevenoaks and Oxted to the west were, respectively, the 10th and 20th wealthiest towns in Britain.

Changing the subject abruptly, I have always been fascinated by the pronunciation of English, as a communicator. My friend Giannina, as an Italian in Britain, once chided me for misunderstanding her on occasion. She made the point, also supported by Michael Skapinker of the *Financial Times*, that foreigners in this country often converse in their own version of English. For instance, "please explain me…" without the intervention of the preposition "to". She told me that this "lingua franca" is perfectly understood by those who come from countries where English is not their first language; additionally, native English speakers would not necessarily understand – and might even be challenged by – pedantics like me. David Crystal in *The Cambridge Encyclopedia of the English Language* (CUP 1994) makes the point, somewhat obliquely, quoting the dialogue in an English Victorian cartoon:

"'Arriet: 'Wot toime his the next troine fer 'Ammersmiff?'
Clerk: 'Due now.'
'Arriet: 'Course Oi dawn't now, stoopid, or Oi wouldn't be harskin' Yer!'"

Clearly, the accent and pronunciation would be unusual today. However, new influences have developed much more recently, notably through the spread of Estuary English. As Crystal explains, the estuary in question is the Lower Thames, and the accent is based on Cockney. It has appeared in many parts of Britain and is partly due to the

FROM PRACTICE TO THEORY

growing importance of London as a transport hub and media capital. Additionally, internal migration has helped to infuse the rest of the country with what some call the "London Whine". (Don't be fazed, Chicagoans have got used to their "honk".) It first gained publicity in a front-page headline in *The Sunday Times* on 14 March 1993. A further recent development is the appearance of the raised last syllable on words such as leader, which now sounds as "leadah" (there could be an Afro-Caribbean influence here). This joins the glottal stop where the "t" is remove from words such as party and motor. A puzzle in London pronunciation is the loss of "gawn", which became an upper-class (U) way of saying "gone" but was originally part of the Cockney demotic. Another interesting change that many Northerners make is to alter their pronunciation of "one" to "won", (as in "gone") where Received Standard would sound as "wan".

Much more significant, I think, is the conversational use of gap-fillers or link phrases such as "you know" and "I mean" and the irritating "sort of". Many news readers start their spiel with "Well..." To be honest, as an ex-lecturer, I was a frequent offender here. Another thing to rant about is the misuse of words to extend their meaning to the off-beam; a recent example was "business literally fell off a cliff" (yes, stock and fittings were found on the beach). The use of "surreal" to indicate "rather unusual" is common; had the user seen a donkey perched on a sewing machine?

The English language, which most Brits are proud of and thankful for, has grown from many sources, notably German, Latin, Greek and American but, importantly, it is always changing naturally to extend our ability to communicate clearly and expressively. Let us hope that

Brexit and our reclaimed "sovereignty" does not encourage any government to launch a protectionist institution to guard our language.

On a connected topic, readers will recall that in Chapter 4, I was asked for my opinion at college on whether a controversial debate should go ahead. The subject had led to Parliamentary sessions and furious articles in British newspapers and concerned the Cyprus insurgency; here a terrorist organisation named EOKA was trying to gain independence from Britain. Two Greek students wished to give the pro-independence side of the dispute. To me, this was clearly another sign of decolonisation, which was in full swing at this time, Ghana being a recent example. The two speakers were not wild-eyed syndicalists but normal, intelligent students pursuing a business degree. As a result, I advised the union president that the event should go ahead as planned. It turned out that it was well attended, was interesting and went well; the subsequent debate was friendly, and the speakers made their point with no rancour demonstrated by either side. This was an acceptable, indeed vital part of student life in a university that was a place where young adults could learn. This learning must embrace both the upside and the downside of disputatious topics; this enables individuals to develop their own judgements. (But does this mean, as Piers Morgan suggests, that everyone should have their own opinion?) On the other hand, I remember at 14 being barred from borrowing certain books by H.G. Wells and other authors, an attitude still probably maintained in some schools today.

This is still a current topic in universities today, much of it imported from the USA. No-platforming and cancel culture are, to me, clear breaches of free speech, which is anti-democratic. If you don't want to hear ideas contrary to your own, you should stay away, switch off. It is no service to intelligent adults to deprive them of new knowledge or, as in many cases, the reinforcement of already received ideas. It also has traces of the policies pursued by Xi in China, Putin in Russia and now in two EU member states. Why don't disruptors just chant "na, na, na" in unison at these events. In this era of apparently extreme disputatiousness, would it not be wonderful to moderate toward a more neutral mindset? For instance, I feel neutral about fox hunting, the Euro, same-sex marriages, the NHS, colonisation and many more topics. I have a sneaking regard for Shakespeare's dictum: "Nothing is either good nor bad, only thinking makes it so". I must confess that I do not subscribe to social media, preferring to subscribe to three hard copy newspapers seven days a week and FV TV and radio for information; for media relaxation, while writing or driving, I listen to Kiss. My landline is security blocked, largely because most of the calls were for my late wife, Liz, who died over 10 years ago, and this I found highly intrusive. The business is now run by my daughter Steph, who has her own website that can field most similar contacts today. My own contact is what I call my "unsmart phone", a little Nokia that can intercept texts.

One thing that does raise my hackles is discourtesy to women, particularly from men. Two examples that affected me personally include an incident in Parliament: my friend Giannina and I were standing next to a visitors group attached to Sir Norman Lamb's East Anglian constituency (Sir Norman is an effective and caring member of his party). A tall man in the group looked at Giannina and asked in a superior and condescending tone who she was! She told me afterwards that she had been shocked by this overt example of what was clearly discriminatory behaviour. Another example involved my wife Liz in Allders department store in Croydon. At this time, I was pushing her in the wheelchair she was confined to after the five hip operations she had undergone. Suddenly, the attitudes that some people, women as well as men, have towards the disabled was revealed.

Where our concern for human life is very important, we should never forget the plenum within which we exist. As mentioned, I have always been interested in astronomy and, latterly, astrophysics, particularly when I received a copy of Fred Hoyle's *The Nature of the Universe* in my teens. On my study notice board, next to the Donne poem, I have the famous ESA photograph taken by the Plank satellite of the remnants of Big Bang and the disk of our galaxy, just one of billions. According to Hoyle, the universe is being continuously created, which could mean a succession of big bangs as it expands and then contracts to a tiny piece of quantum energy (oops!). A much more immediate and fascinating question is why we have never knowingly encountered aliens. The standard explanations range from most civilisations blowing themselves up or otherwise declining before they have solved the means of long-range interstellar travel. My own theory was that it was the unimaginable distances between star clusters and galaxies. For example, it would take years to reach our nearest star, Proxima Centauri, even travelling at half a billion miles an hour (faster than light) in an FLT ship.

FROM PRACTICE TO THEORY

But new research from Southampton University (*The Daily Telegraph*, 3 January 2021) suggests that it has been pure luck that Earth has continued to exist with a life-support system; by modelling the key elements that determine climate trends in a large population of planets, it was concluded that finding one in the Goldilocks Zone that Earth inhabits was highly improbable. So much for the greatest aspect of the meaning of things. As Rod Liddle recently observed: we are effectively, alone.

Back to tangibility, toward the end of my stint at broker Scott Goff Hancock, Roger Nicholas, an associate of the firm who often popped in to sound out our views, approached me privately on my assessment of inflation over the next five years. Part of our job as analysts was, at the start of market trading, to attend to the research partner who went through our massed ranks in front of our monitor screens to ask what our individual estimates of market performance were; this boiled down to "buy", "sell" or "hold", and the process was aided by everyone having purchased the *Financial Times* (paid for by the firm for our perusal on the train). Inflation was, at the time, very concerning, due to the oil crisis. For the previous year (1976), it had hit an unprecedented 26 per cent. I hazarded that over the next two years it would fall by around 5 percentage points, and this turned out to be correct, even though OPEC had engineered a further hike in the UK oil price. What we had not foreseen (unlike my prediction of the 1990 recession) was the 1980 economic downturn. This, in typical cyclical fashion, was followed by the 1980s boom, particularly in the retail sector, where extensive new product development helped. This could have contributed to the false belief among retailers, particularly Marks & Spencer, that the future was a forever growth. A Channel 4 documentary screened in 1994 superbly captured the hubris of the time. Entitled *The World According to St Michael*, the in-bred arrogance of its culture was on show until the fall of 1998. Over 20 years later, it is still not properly recovered. But who can we turn to for effective ideas? When he was Chancellor of the Exchequer, Denis Healey (now the late Lord Healey) remarked that security analysts in city broking houses were mostly "teenage scribblers" fresh out of Oxbridge, with brilliant minds and good degrees but with little idea of how managers coped in the real world. The implication was that older and more experienced analysts could offer well thought out and practical advice to investors. One case that suggests the opposite is that of Gerald Horner, a well-known veteran analyst employed by Scrimgeour Vickers. In 1985, he convinced the then management of Asda that the UK food sector would saturate within 10 years – accurately, as it turned out. His recommendation was that the supermarket group should merge with MFI, a flat-pack furniture retailer. This would provide economies of scale and scope, a defensive strategy that would reduce competitive risk. His rationale was that both firms had close similarities in the way they did business. The problem was that they were in totally different businesses – food and durables – and more critically, their cultures were at variance; no strategic fit. Asda was rescued by Walmart, and MFI expired largely due to the skills of IKEA. (This is based on a case I wrote for *The Changing Face of British Retailing*, Newman Books, 1987. It was subsequently rejected by various leading publishers as part of a major work of mine entitled – perhaps too provocatively – *Strategy is just Planning*. Nobody said publishers had a sense of humour.)

At the time of writing, Brexit has finally occurred, and everyone is wondering what the outcome will be for the economy. This was particularly salient, because the UK was still suffering from the Covid-19 epidemic and awaiting the essential vaccination programme. From an economic point of view, inflation has been stuck at around 2 per cent for a long time, matched with near-zero interest levels. Some Brexit supporters seem to think that we shall see a repeat of the "Roaring Twenties" of the last century. This looks a little trite, based on history repeating itself; some observers have reminded us of what happened at the end of that decade. On the other hand, although the economy has suffered an estimated fall of 8 per cent in its GDP due to Covid, a substantial recovery is due, not only from vaccine distribution but from its exceptional flexibility. Remember the rebound after Black Wednesday, when the pound fell out of the EMS in 1992, and more recently after the 2008 financial crisis. At the time, official forecasts were dire. Why do these people adopt such gloomy prognoses? It is the easy way out – of hedging bets by proclaiming a disaster, aided by a large dose of groupthink. In expectation terms, many people fear the worst; when it doesn't happen, they are relieved and soon forget the error. Economists like myself, however, express annoyance and generally go unheard. We try to explain the error by blaming the establishment's out-dated models, based on inelastic criteria and a misunderstanding of how important market participant behaviour is on the fundamentals, supply and demand – the mysterious sentiment factor (illustrated by my Gulf War example discussed previously). Perhaps we should all become lucky contrarians.

For the first quarter century of life, I avoided smoking. There were rumours at school in the 1950s that showed the depredations that impose on lungs and other organs. We were not offered these as part of the curriculum, and television was a one-channel show that virtually no one had access to. Even in the army in Germany, where a tin of 25 Benson & Hedges tipped cost one shilling and two pence halfpenny at the NAAFI, I was not attracted. It was only when I joined Littlewoods at the Edinburgh store in Princes Street that I took up the habit. Virtually every member of the staff smoked. At breaks, not smoking made one something of a social misfit; so inevitably began a habit which lasted for the next 30 or so years. They say that it takes seven attempts to stop. I never counted, but when I did, it was not due to any medicinal solution or even the application of iron self-discipline; it was a persistent, dry little cough. It was irritation, perhaps underlined by fear, which released me without any serious withdrawal problems.

Alcohol was different. My family was teetotal, as well as non-smokers. I suspect my father had the occasional sherry while away preaching in Blairgowrie, or wherever. Smoking, of course, is just silly; but alcohol is a wonderland of different flavours, power levels, colours, smells and even bottles and labels. Its distinctiveness as a commodity has significant social purport; this accretes to class, fashion and to time and place. To my mind, it was closely associated with dinner parties. Looking over my personal diaries over the past 40 years, the 1970s, 1980s and early 1990s show that at home we hosted what we might call "proper" dinner parties at least once a fortnight. These involved varied pre-drinks, at least four courses, two decent wines, with port, brandy and "ladies' drinks" like Cointreau and Tia Maria afterwards; in those days, ostentatious crystalware was standard. The rest of the time, "returns" involved being invited to the houses of perhaps 30 or so friends. Liz's reputation as a Cordon Bleu trained chef helped produce great competition and very high standards amongst our friends' cooking – some of the women had also been professional cooks, of course. Today, as a retired widower, I have suppers alone or with one friend (partly due to Covid). Until recently, with half a dozen male friends in a pub was a great way to spend lunch; we would start off with craft beers, like Brewdog's "Punk" or real ales such as Harvey's, Young's or Shepherd Neame's, because we live in the South East. This would be followed by a decent Macon, preferably Lugny. My old, sadly departed friend Bill McLean was a bit of a Guinness connoisseur; he once told me that the company had developed a "Winter" variant because the black stuff had the habit of going off during very hot summers (today, the "cool" version obviates this problem). In 1982, I was in Dublin for a Marketing Education Group conference and took time off to visit the St James's Brewery. Instead of the expected tour of the brewery, we were shown a video instead; this was hosted by a Wogan-voiced presenter who said things like: "Now in true Irish style, we'll start at the end…" Afterwards, in the bar upstairs, we were allowed to sample the product, under the auspices of who we were told were directors of the company. I queried one of these gentlemen about the winter variant and he vociferously denied that this adulteration took place. This begged two questions: did the stout deteriorate in hot weather and, if so, was it poured away? Out of courtesy, I did not pursue them, but the subsequent introduction of cooled Guinness must have solved any problem that might have existed. My disappointment was compounded, as a then smoker, when I entered a tobacconist to ask for a packet of Guards cigarettes. Unfortunately, Bobby Sands had just died in Maze Prison after his hunger strike. Noting my English accent, the proprietor refused to serve me.

Women. Although I had several girlfriends over my time in London, most, except Sandra, were casual. In any case, I was in a stage between breaking up with Heather and meeting with Liz, my wife. At no time during this 10-year interim did I see any woman as someone I longed to make a life partner. If a woman did not succumb to my charms, I would never, ever try to break her, and certainly never think of rape. I truly cannot understand how men can harm women. How to tackle this epidemic of hate? The current government proposals at the time of writing seem confused. I did put candles in my windows a week after the horrific murder of Sarah Everard.

I had just started to edit this MS when I had a dream, indeed, a nightmare. I dream every night, often in full colour. Occasionally, they involve gorgeous young women, tying in with Sigmund Freud's interpretations, which I read when I was 18; this was the time when you were reading everything unconnected with your degree. Anyway, the editing process brought back many aspects of the mish-mash that was my career, particularly my obsession with the concept of strategy. In the dream, I had organised a conference on the subject, entitled "Strategy is just Planning". This phrase was a quotation from a young FE teacher at a meeting in the ill-fated Greenwich School of Management. At one point, the guileless woman had declared that every time a student asked for a definition of the word strategy, she replied "Oh, it's just planning!" Readers will remember that this was the title of one of my rejected MS. The first chapter was devoted to the mis-use of the term; it is often deployed, particularly by government ministers, as meaning "tactics" – how to pursue an overarching aim, rather than what the objective actually is: achieving total herd immunity in a population (tactical options: AstraZeneca or Pfizer?).

Back to the dream: after booking the venue and advertising the event, I found myself in a huge low-ceilinged and carpeted room, sitting at a very large round table facing a dozen punters. I had adopted Open University techniques to encourage non-threatening participation, by jokingly introducing myself and obtaining participant self-identification all round. I opened up with the simple question "What is strategy?" and this started a lively discussion. While this was going on, a crowd of casually-dressed people moved in, carrying tables and chairs and forming themselves into discussion groups. Soon the room was filled with a chatting throng of hundreds. In a short time, they began to encroach upon each other, and disputes over space and noise levels began; this intensified into fisticuffs at some points. I hastily got up to find a management office and walked into an ante-room; this was filled with more people, like me searching for someone to sort out the chaos. It turned out that the groups were many and varied: flat-earthers, UFO sighters, no-platformers, capital-punishers, cyber-mercenaries, groups that refused to identify themselves, and others who clearly did not know why they were there. I was, of course, unable to find anyone who could calm the situation, and then I woke up. I can guarantee that, like everything written in this memoir, is entirely true.

I have thoroughly enjoyed writing this autobiography and hope that my family, friends and any dear readers will enjoy it, even though it has ended on a serious note. Serious is as serious does, and hopefully the tone of the memoir suggests that one of my self-identifiers is being silly as well.

APPENDIX

Quiz

At no extra cost, we have thrown in a quotations, alternative answer quiz, with help from J.M. and M.J. Cohen's *The Penguin Dictionary of Modern Quotations*, Penguin Books, 1971. The idea is based on a quiz I produced for an extended family Christmas holiday 10 years ago, when we filled two large barns in Norfolk

WHO SAID WHAT?.

1 The lady's not for burning. (a) Margaret Thatcher; (b) Christopher Fry; (c) Joan of Arc.
2 Just when we were beginning to win the match, our inside left has scored against his own side. (a) Tiny Rowland; (b) Clement Attlee; (c) Alex Ferguson.
3 Not many people know that. (a) Peter Sellers; (b) Michael Caine; (c) Chris Grayling.
4 Something must be done. (a) Edward VIII; (b) David Cameron; (c) Steve Jobs.
5 I caught a cold in the park – the gate was open. (a) Paul Simon; (b) Ernie Wise; (c) James Joyce.
6 Mustard's no good without roast beef. (a) Groucho Marx; (b) Chico Marx; (c) Jamie Oliver.

7 I have never made a firebrand speech. (a) Donald Trump; (b) Winston Churchill; (c) Adolf Hitler.

8 Blessed are the cheesemakers. (a) Paul Bresson; (b) Monty Python; (c) Stuart Rose.

9 The law of the jungle is the oldest law in the world. (a) Al Capone; (b) Nelson Mandela; (c) Rudyard Kipling.

10 I can't drink Guinness from a thick mug. I can only drink it from a thin glass. (a) Harold Pinter. (b) Brian Behan; (c) Terry Wogan.

11 I don't believe in morality. I'm a disciple of Bernard Shaw. (a) Jeffrey Epstein; (b) G.B. Shaw; (c) D.H. Lawrence.

12 Much as he is opposed to law-breaking, he is not bigoted about it. (a) The Secret Barrister; (b) Philip Green; (c) Damon Runyon.

13 Television? No good will come of this device. The word is half Greek and half Latin. (a) Lord Reith; (b) C.P. Scott; (c) T.S. Eliot

14 Comedy, like sodomy, is an unnatural act. (a) The Archbishop of York; (b) Marty Feldman; (c) Peter Tatchell.

15 Exercise is important. It's important for peoples' health and well-being. And that equally applies to exercise. (a) Ivor Cutler; (b) Priti Patel; (c) Charles Atlas.

16 Other nations use 'force'. We Britons alone use 'Might'. (a) Nigel Farage; (b) Anthony Eden; (c) Evelyn Waugh.

17 New York's a small place when it comes to the part of it that wakes up when the rest are going to bed (a) Frank Sinatra; (b) P.G. Wodehouse; (c) Andy Warhol.

18 Wakey, wakey, rise and shine. (a) Billy Graham; (b) Harry Hill; (c) Billy Cotton.
19 Like Webster's dictionary, we're Morocco-bound. (a) Jan Morris; (b) Bing Crosby; (c) Paul Hamlyn.
20 Such as I am, I cannot fail to be, at a given moment, at the centre of the stage. (a) Gregg Wallace; (b) General de Gaulle; (c) Nicola Sturgeon.
21 The rest of the world most certainly does not owe us a living. (a) Charlotte Church; (b) The Duke of Edinburgh; (c) David Attenborough.
22 I never hated a man enough to give him his diamonds back. (a) Marilyn Monroe; (b) Cheryl Cole; (c) Zsa Zsa Gabor.
23 The land of my fathers? My fathers can have it! (a) Leon Trotsky; (b) Jeremy Corbyn; (c) Dylan Thomas.
24 We will bury you. (a) The Archbishop of Canterbury; (b) Nikita Khrushchev; (c) Hermann Göring.
25 Nowadays the old prison has been turned into a first-class hotel, with a service which any Michelin Guide would be only too pleased to condemn. (a) Spike Milligan; (b) Trip Advisor; (c) Eric Morecambe.
26 How can you expect to think in anything but a negative way when you have got chronic intestinal poisoning? (a) Aldous Huxley; (b) George Orwell; (c) Evelyn Waugh.
27 I'll give you a definite maybe. (a) Boris Johnson; (b) Sam Goldwyn; (c) Michael Fish.
28 The maxim of the British people is 'business as usual'. (a) Harold Macmillan. (b) Theresa May; (c) Winston Churchill.
29 Eating people is wrong. (a) Michael Flanders; (b) The Pope; (c) Malcolm Bradbury.

30 We are on a glide path to oblivion. (a) The Governor of the Bank of England; (b) Tony Hancock; (c) Steve Jobs.
31 A man who has a million dollars is as well off as if he were rich. (a) Nick Clegg; (b) Sheldon Adelson; (c) John Jacob Astor III.
32 Bugger Bognor. (a) George V; (b) Sir Harry Lauder; (c) Friedrich Nietzsche.
33 Nothing to be done. (a) William Shakespeare; (b) Samuel Beckett; (c) Judas Iscariot.
34 Call down that brasstitute. (a) Brendan Behan; (b) James Joyce. (c) Dominic Behan.
35 Spiritually, I was at Eton. (a) Oscar Wilde; (b) John Betjeman; (c) Ian Hislop.
36 Life is rather like a tin of sardines – we're all of us looking for the key. (a) John Cleese; (b) Eric Chitty; (c) Alan Bennett.
37 Judy! Judy! Judy! (a) Vincente Minnelli; (b) Cary Grant; (c) James Mason.
38 Truth is never pure and rarely simple. (a) Pontius Pilate; (b) Oscar Wilde; (c) Lord Pearson.
39 It's all any reasonable child can expect if the dad is present at the conception. (a) Sir Herbert Read; (b) Joe Orton; (c) Kingsley Amis.
40 As an artist, a man has no home in Europe, save in Paris. (a) Friedrich Nietzsche; (b) Henry Miller; (c) George Orwell.
41 An actor's a guy who, if you ain't talking about him, he ain't listening. (a) Trevor Nunn; (b) Marlon Brando; (c) Richard Harris.
42 Never put a baby on a hot slab; (a) Dr Spock; (b) Anonymous; (c) Hank Janson.

43 I'm walking backwards for Christmas. (a) Michael Bentine; (b) Spike Milligan; (c) Peter Sellers.
44 Hello Playmates! (a) Tommy Cooper; (b) Arthur Askey: (c) Tommy Handley.
45 Anybody who hates children and likes dogs can't be all bad. (a) Yoko Ono; (b) General Franco; (c) W.C. Fields
46 You've never had it so good. (a) Donald Trump; (b) Harold Macmillan; (c) Henry Ford.
47 Include me out. (a) Arthur Miller; (b) Samuel Goldwyn; (c) George Gershwin.
48 I never forget a face, but I'll make an exception in your case. (a) Karl Marx; (b) Jeremy Clarkson; (c) Groucho Marx.
49 The ballot is stronger than the bullet. (a) Maxim Litvinov; (b) Harold Wilson; (c) Abraham Lincoln.
50 He is a clear and present danger to the country we love. (a) Joe Biden; (b) Lauren Boebert; (c)Nancy Pelosi.

The answers are shown in the traditional way below, before revealing an interesting sidelight: having analysed the content of the main *Penguin Dictionary of Quotations*, also authored by the Cohens, less than 5 per cent of entries are from female writers. This discrepancy is emphasised by the huge number of entries from major literary works such as the Bible and Shakespeare's output. All this, of course, has nothing to do with the scholarly and painstaking work of the two compilers, but perhaps to the attitudes of publishers and literary agents. Although there is nothing in the entry for George Eliot in my copy of *The Oxford*

Companion, for her name change, she may have had the same thought as, more recently, the author of the *Harry Potter* series.

QUIZ ANSWERS

1 b 2 b 3 a 4 a 5 c 6 b 7 b 8 b 9 c 10 a 11 b
12 c 13 b 14 b 15 b 16 c 17 c 18 c 19 b 20 b
21 b 22 c 23 c 24 b 25 a 26 a 27 b 28 c 29 c
30 c 31 c 32 a 33 b 34 a 35 b 36 c 37 b 38 b
39 b 40 a 41 b 42 b 43 b 44 b 45 c 46 b 47 b
48 c 49 c 50 c

BIBLIOGRAPHY

Ackroyd, Peter. London: The Biography, Chatto and Windus, 2000
Bootle, Roger. The Death of Inflation, Nicholas Brealey Publishing, 1997
Cohen J.M. and Cohen M.J., The Penguin Dictionary of Quotations, Penguin Books, 1963
Cohen J.M. and Cohen M.J., The Penguin Dictionary of Modern Quotations, Penguin Books, 1978
Cohen J.M. and Cohen M.J. (Compiled by Robert Stewart), The Penguin Dictionary of Political Quotations, Penguin Books, 1984.
Cox, Roger. Retail Site Assessment, Business Books, 1968
Cox, Roger. Retail Development, Business Books, 1972
Cox, Roger. Retailing, M&E Handbooks, 1978
Cox, Roger. Running Your Own Shop, Kogan Page, 1985
Cox, Roger & Brittain, Paul. Retailing: An Introduction (5th Edition), FT Prentice Hall 2004
Crystal, David. The Cambridge Encyclopedia of the English Language, CUP, 1995
Euromonitor: Retail and Distribution Surveys – Voluntary Chains and Buying Groups 1988
Firth, Michael. Investment Analysis, Harper & Row, 1975
Geraghty, Tony. BRIXMIS, Harper Collins, 1997

Goleman, Daniel. Emotional Intelligence, Bloomsbury, 1995

Herman, Arthur. The Scottish Enlightenment, Fourth Estate, 2001

Hoyle, Fred. The Nature of the Universe, Basil Blackwell, 1950

Inwood, Stephen. A History of London, Macmillan, 2000

Jarrold Short Walks – Kent, Jarrold Publishing, 2003

Johnson, Gerry et al. Exploring Strategy (11th Edition), FT Prentice Hall, 2017

Kay, John. The Business of Economics, OUP, 1996

MacInnes, Colin. London: City of Any Dream, Readers' Union, Thames and Hudson, 1963

McClelland, William. Costs and Competition in Retailing, Macmillan, 1966

McFadyen, Edward (Editor), the Changing Face of British Retailing, Newman Books, 1987.

The Menzies Group. John Menzies (Holdings) Ltd., 1965

Mintel. Retail Intelligence, Volume 1, 1995

NEDO, Distributive Trades EDC, Urban Models in Shopping Studies, 1970

Rand McNally, The Road Atlas – US, Canada, Mexico, Latest Edition

Reilly, William. The Law of Retail Gravitation, New York, 1931

Taleb, Nassim Nicholas. The Black Swan, Penguin Books, 2007

Tett, Gillian. The Silo Effect, Abacus, 2015

The Writers' Directory 1988–90 (8th Edition), St James Press, 1988

Tvede, Lars. Business Cycles, Harwood Academic Publishers, 1997

Schumpeter, Joseph. Business Cycles, Porcupine Press, 1989

Smith, David. The Age of Instability, Profile Books, 2010

Vinen, Richard. National Service: Conscription in Britain, Allen Lane, 2014

West, Alan (Editor), Handbook of British Retailing, Gower, 1988.

Who's Who in the World, Marquis

The Oxford Companion to English Literature, edited by Margaret Drabble, OUP 1985

NOTES

www.ingramcontent.com/pod-product-compliance
Lightning Source LLC
Chambersburg PA
CBHW040256170426
43192CB00020B/2823